Praise for *To Make and Keep Peace Among Ourselves and with All Nations*

"Angelo Codevilla makes clear that peace is not preordained. There once was a popular advertisement 'When E. F. Hutton speaks we listen.' When Angelo Codevilla writes *To Make and Keep Peace*, we listen."

J. WILLIAM MIDDENDORF II, Secretary of the Navy, 1974–1977

"*To Make and Keep Peace* is an eloquent and deeply thoughtful reflection upon the greatest issue of statecraft, war and peace. It is distilled from a career in academia and high levels of government service. Angelo Codevilla has the breadth and depth of experience combined with the intellectual horsepower to understand the dynamics of international power and politics and to see clearly what must be done to avoid repeating the tragic blunders of history. Most importantly he has a precise yet fluid style that engages specialist and nonspecialist alike."

JOHN LEHMAN, Secretary of the Navy, 1981–1987
and Member of the 9/11 Commission

"Codevilla has invented a new category of policy analysis: brilliant common sense. The product of deep learning, this invaluable book argues that we can only subordinate war to authentic needs if we first understand how peace is achieved and sustained. A splendid parry to our ruling establishment's suicidal fantasies, Codevilla's steely logic slices through the knot of self-defeating policies foisted upon us by those who refuse to confront the challenges of our age with intellectual—or moral—integrity."

RALPH PETERS, Fox News Strategic Analyst and author of
*Lines of Fire: A Renegade Writes on Strategy,
Intelligence, and Security* and *Cain at Gettysburg*

"Codevilla's new book is an original, brash, and invaluable perspective on the relationship of war and peace in American history—and more generally."

CARNES LORD, Professor of Strategic Leadership, US Naval War College

To Make and Keep

PEACE

Among Ourselves and with All Nations

The Hoover Institution gratefully acknowledges the following individuals and foundations for their significant support of the Working Group on the Role of Military History in Contemporary Conflict

VICTOR AND KAREN TRIONE

WILLARD AND MARGARET CARR

THE LYNDE AND HARRY BRADLEY FOUNDATION

To Make and Keep
PEACE
Among Ourselves and with All Nations

Angelo M. Codevilla

HOOVER INSTITUTION PRESS

STANFORD UNIVERSITY   STANFORD, CALIFORNIA

www.hoover.org

Hoover Institution Press Publication No. 645

Hoover Institution at Leland Stanford Junior University,
Stanford, California 94305-6010

First printing 2014
20 19 18 17 16 15 14   7 6 5 4 3 2 1

Manufactured in the United States of America

The paper used in this publication meets the minimum Requirements of the American National Standard for Information Sciences—Permanence of Paper for Printed Library Materials, ANSI/NISO Z39.48-1992. ♾

Cataloging-in-Publication Data is available from the Library of Congress.
ISBN: 978-0-8179-1714-2 (cloth. : alk. paper)
ISBN: 978-0-8179-1715-9 (pbk. : alk. paper)
ISBN: 978-0-8179-1716-6 (epub)
ISBN: 978-0-8179-1717-3 (mobi)
ISBN: 978-0-8179-1718-0 (PDF)

To Ann
my very own Beatrice

The Lord bless thee and keep thee
The Lord make his face to shine upon thee and be gracious
unto thee
The Lord lift up his countenance upon thee
     And give thee peace.

Numbers 6:24–26

. . . to do all which may achieve and cherish a just and lasting
peace among ourselves and with all nations.

Abraham Lincoln

Peace is the highest aspiration of the American people.

Ronald Reagan

Contents

Foreword

To Make and Keep Peace Among Ourselves and with All Nations is being published under the auspices of the Hoover Institution Press in connection with the Working Group on the Role of Military History in Contemporary Conflict, of which Angelo Codevilla is a member and whose mission is reflected in explaining current crises through study of the wars of the past. Codevilla is perhaps best known to the reading public for two influential works—the coauthored *War: Ends and Means* (with the late Paul Seabury) and, more recently, *The Ruling Class*. Those two books provide a proper introduction to *To Make and Keep Peace Among Ourselves and with All Nations*.

The first, *War: Ends and Means* is a historical survey of how wars begin, are often waged, and why they either end successfully in peace or lead to further instability and conflicts. The work proved an insightful, if not blunt, reminder that utopian pacifism and idealistic internationalism more often provoke and prolong conflicts than ensure peace. In contrast, a more lasting settlement follows when war's prime aim is to defeat the enemy, discredit its cause, and remove the political conditions that led to acts of aggression in the first place.

Grandiose notions of nation-building, democracy spreading, and international governance become mere slogans, if a power does not first focus on what it wants from its resort to arms, whether it has the necessary means to achieve its military aims, and whether it possesses a clear idea of the desired contours of the postwar landscape. Implicit in Codevilla's argument was a paradox: the increasing military power of modern affluent democracies is accompanied by a growing misunderstanding about and even misuse of such preeminent force. More precisely, the more powerful we become, the less confident we are in using power for national, much less moral, interests.

The Ruling Class offered a bookend domestic argument to *War: Ends and Means* that echoed many of these same tragic themes. Our twenty-first-century American coastal elite—prepped at tony universities, shaped by postmodern relativism, trusting in a huge government overseen by a self-appointed technocracy, exempt often from the practical ramifications of their own starry-eyed ideology, and deeply skeptical of traditional American values—has captured the reins of power of both American political parties, not to mention the media, foundations, universities, and the arts.

This cultural nexus often has little empathy for traditional American protocols, at least as defined by limited government, the influence of Judeo-Christian religion, and rugged individualism and personal liberty rather than a mandated equality of result. The elite, at least in theory, apparently prefers to see America as either unexceptional or exceptionally out of tune with preferable notions of democratic socialism abroad.

Codevilla now combines the arguments of these two prior diverse works into his latest reflection about how *To Make and Keep Peace Among Ourselves and with All Nations*. His argument is again unapologetic and straightforward. Despite unprecedented military power, America is fighting more wars abroad than ever and winning almost none of them, much less improving American stature in the world or its ability to help our friends and punish our enemies. Such confusion is largely the result of the flawed ideas of the "ruling class." Without a learned approach to the past's stern lessons, and knowledge of timeless human nature, the ruling elite frenetically jumps from one conflict to another, rarely with clear ideas of what our interests are, and thus without any notion of the means necessary to achieve our ends. Certainly, our latest experience in Afghanistan and Iraq, and especially American misadventures during the Arab Spring in our efforts in Egypt, Libya, and Syria, bear out Codevilla's warnings that we contemplate social and political quick fixes without first ensuring that we have defeated and discredited the enemy—to the degree we can even agree on who he is.

Codevilla quotes liberally from primary texts of a long Western literary and philosophical tradition, emphasizing both the unchanging nature of mankind and thus the need for a tragic acceptance of war's unchanging laws. He then illustrates the abstract and theoretical with relevant allusions to major wars in Western history, while driving home contemporary lessons by direct allusions to America's most recent misadventures of the post-9/11 era.

Codevilla concludes by lamenting two contemporary trends that sum up America's deviation from the Founders' nation of limited government and their warnings about intervening abroad either indecisively or for interests not directly our own. Nation-building assumes that America first has defeated the enemy, forced him to accept our superiority, and has the know-how to implant democracy among peoples without previous experiences of consensual government. In theory that might work with sufficient force; in fact, it usually has not.

Meanwhile at home, fears over homeland security have created a government octopus. It too often sucks up vast resources, while curbing civil rights, and empowering government bureaucracies, largely because of a therapeutic reluctance to identify our Islamist enemies and take the focused and often narrow measures needed to protect society from them.

Codevilla's message may strike some as pessimistic, given his acceptance of the ubiquity of war and his warnings about the tendency of wealthier Westerners to believe that their money, education, and high-mindedness exempt them from the darker ramifications of human nature. In fact, his book is an upbeat reminder of how the benefits of peace are critical to the human experience, and why it is so crucial to achieve them in this troubled and confused age of Western self-doubt.

Read *To Make and Keep Peace* to appreciate how our best-intended efforts at peace have too often ensured war—and why that is neither a noble nor useful development.

Victor Davis Hanson
Martin and Illie Anderson Senior Fellow, Classics/Military History
Chairman, the Working Group on the Role of
Military History in Contemporary Conflict
The Hoover Institution, Stanford University

Acknowledgments

This book is the first fruit of a 2005 grant from the Earhart Foundation to study how early American thought on international affairs bears on current problems. Coming as it did at a time of my physical debility, the grant demonstrated confidence in me. I thank Victor Davis Hanson for his kind attention to the manuscript, and fellowship to a fellow fan of the ancients. I am grateful to Jameson Campaigne for continuing to teach me more about publishing than I ever wanted to know, beginning when he published my first book at Open Court Press in 1974.

Preface

Achieving "a just and lasting peace among ourselves and with all nations" is statesmanship's proper goal. It is also naturally indivisible, because peace with foreigners guards tranquility among fellow citizens and nothing so incites domestic strife and fosters the loss of liberty as do war's despotic necessities. Domestic harmony is as precarious as it is precious, everywhere. But nowhere as much as in America, our "nation of many nations," where so much diversity offers so much occasion for division. Nor are any people so jealous of liberty as are Americans. Fear of war's effect on peace and liberty at home is the reason why our founding statesmen, beginning with George Washington, were willing to sacrifice so much for peace and agonized so deeply over war.

Among later generations of statesmen, however, other concerns gradually obscured that healthy caution. The illusion of serving noble causes by making foreign quarrels our own has lured the past century's statesmen to abandon their predecessors' sharp distinction between war and peace and to fight wars mindless of war's first principle: that it is an extraordinary event conceived to end in peace.

The result, intended to be ordinary and permanent, has been violent "nation-building" abroad plus "homeland security" in America, enforced by a national security–homeland security complex whose very size fits it for use as an instrument of partisan strife. "Peace among ourselves and with all nations" is beyond the horizon of twenty-first-century American statesmen.

The purpose of this book is to recover understanding of peace as the practical lodestar by which the American people and statesmen may navigate domestic as well as international affairs on any given day. In these affairs, which include preparing for wars and all too often fighting them, the compass of peace is the surest guide. What is to be America's peace? How is it to be won and preserved in our time?

Peace is statesmanship's natural focus. Our civilization teaches that all human activity aims at some end natural to itself. Plato reminds us of the obvious: shoes are the proper end of shoemaking, and food is the natural end of farming. What, he asks, is the natural, the proper product of the statesman if not fostering man's highest, most peculiar functions? Aristotle, echoed by St. Augustine, wrote that victory—the establishment of one's own peace—is the natural end of war. War itself may be understood only in terms of the peace from which it starts and of the peace in which it ends. Just as farmers plow not for the sake of plowing but for specific crops, real statesmen fight wars not for the sake of fighting but rather to achieve the peace that suits them, or to avoid the enemy's version of peace. In the end, some peace there must be.

Because peace is the precondition for enjoying the good things of life, peace must be statecraft's proximate objective. The United States of America, by virtue of its size, strength, and location, has unusually great latitude for determining what kind of peace it can choose for itself. Pity that American statesmen in the past hundred years have given so little thought to what is to be America's peace.

Since the turn of the twentieth century, American statesmen and academics have so focused on abolishing war in general, have sponsored so many "peace processes," and have so supported or opposed all manner of causes that they have diverted attention from earning our peace in any particular circumstance—from ending *this* war, to avoiding *that* war. Often do our statesmen contemplate commitments to conflicts, but seldom how to end them in ways that benefit the American people.

Paradigmatically, President Woodrow Wilson opposed entry into the Great War while opposing efforts to end it unless and until he saw what he imagined an opportunity to craft perpetual peace; similarly, Franklin Roosevelt characterized the onset of World War II as an impersonal "epidemic," and then aimed America's war at abolishing humanity's "ancient evils, ancient ills." By such generalities have our statesmen avoided their responsibility for America's peace.

In our time, inattention to what peace is and what it requires is all the more remarkable because, in the past hundred years, Americans have enjoyed it only during two brief periods (1919–41, 1992–2001). Since 9/11, the American body politic seems to have come to terms with its leaders' contention (never argued fully) that henceforth the permanent, normal state of life defies dictionary definitions of war and peace.

The dictionary is the least of things that our time is supposed to have repealed. The US government's academic venues (and most universities) teach that, since war is diplomacy by violent means, human intercourse is a seamless continuum between garden-variety business and mutual destruction—that there is no clear line between peace and war. This Cliff Notes version of Carl von Clausewitz has deprived many otherwise thoughtful Americans of the capacity to distinguish peace from war.

Mainstream American statesmen and academics no longer think about how to restore peace, in part because they have invested mind, heart, and personal interest—as well as the nation's blood and treasure—in the quarrels of countless contending states and parties all over the globe. While it is difficult to tell on which side of these contests lies the American people's interest, if any, or how, when, or whether any contest might end, it is beyond doubt that the US government's involvement has resulted in more hostility and less respect for America on the part of some if not all of the nations and parties involved.

The resulting dynamic recalls Pericles's warning to war-weary Athenians that "to recede is no longer possible," because "the animosities incurred in the exercise [of empire] . . . is the lot of all who have aspired to rule others."

We cannot know whether America can ever live in peace again, what kind of peace we may win for ourselves, or what peace we may end up having to endure. But we do know that our statesmen and academics have ceased even to think about such things. Our purpose is to rekindle such thoughts.

Our statesmen and academics befog the realities of peace and war, victory and defeat, with intellectual oxymorons such as "exit strategy." Nevertheless, they make clear that the new, permanent state of non-peace, non-war grants them the discretionary powers that pertain logically to military commanders in the face of enemies-in-arms. But if military discretion—inherently unlimited and despotic—is to be forever untethered to any operation or to any outcome, if neither victory nor peace is ever again to be, then war powers have become the ordinary rule of life among ourselves. If so, the contemporary invocation of war powers creates a wholly new, short constitution: rulers may do whatever they can get away with at home and abroad now and forevermore.

Exemplar of this constitution, Section 1021 of the National Defense Authorization Act of 2011, purports to empower the president to designate any American as an enemy, to hold him incommunicado indefinitely, or to kill him. This constitution is surely alien to that of 1789, conceived by and for a people living ordinarily in peace and liberty, and waging war occasionally. Hence, the post-9/11 hostilities—or at least the manner of thinking about and waging them that we have uncritically adopted—seem to have defeated the very idea of limited government, as well as of peace.

To whose benefit, to whose detriment will our increasingly unlimited government's powers be put? Answering that question calls forth ever-more violent partisan strife. That reality calls us to consider anew what it will take for us to restore our peace.

The post-9/11 hostilities having left some 30,000 Americans crippled for life, private groups have nobly undertaken to raise money to palliate their condition. One of their solicitations is accompanied by a plaintive song that asks Americans to "say a prayer for peace." Surely, prayer to God is in order always and everywhere. But earthly peace is one of those earthly goods the production of which we reasonably expect from the persons whom we hire to produce them. Had we been paying plumbers to fix our house's pipes, praying God to stop continuing leaks would bespeak severe judgment on the plumbers. Praying for peace after our statesmen have spent trillions of dollars and killed uncounted thousands without producing peace acknowledges that those statesmen and their "bench" in the universities and think tanks either don't know how to produce it, or have other priorities.

Relief from such experts begins with firing them. Relief requires understanding the problem enough to hire persons who will do the job. This book is to supply that understanding

Our statesmen's insufficiencies transcend the intellectual realm. That realm itself is beyond our scope here. So is statesmanship as a whole. This book merely reestablishes Western civilization's, and specifically American statecraft's, understanding of peace, what it takes to make it and keep it. Specifically, it reminds Americans of why, precisely, our founding generation placed the pursuit of peace ahead of all other objectives, excepting the "quiet and peaceable life in all godliness and honesty" that they believed peace would allow the American people to live.

This book shows how they tried to keep the peace, how they distinguished peace from war, and how their successors came to confuse peace and war. It then provides intellectual guidelines for reestablishing the distinction between the two.

John Quincy Adams ended his 1821 celebration of American statecraft with: "Go ye and do likewise." Whoever might wish in our time to refocus American statecraft on peace might well take from this book's description of the past century an equally succinct exordium: "Look ye and do pretty close to the opposite."

The text that follows is replete with references to and quotes from primary sources. I have placed in the text information sufficient, in our electronic age, for the reader easily to delve into the source material. The text is followed by a list of some of the most important books and articles cited or referred to, or that I especially recommend as background.

Angelo M. Codevilla
January 2014

To Make and Keep
PEACE
Among Ourselves and with All Nations

Introduction

"...peace among ourselves and with all nations"

By these final words carved in his memorial, Abraham Lincoln underlined the belief of America's founders that securing peace is our Union's primordial job. Knowing that foreign wars and strife among fellow citizens exacerbate and lead from one to the other, Alexander Hamilton, James Madison, and John Jay devoted the *Federalist Papers'* first section to peace. In our time, American statesmen seem to have forgotten. This book aims to recall the simple truth that "peace among ourselves and with all nations" is statesmanship's first goal, and hence that its chief question must be: "What is to be our peace?"

As St. Augustine wrote in the fifth century AD, even pirates crave peace among themselves if only to enjoy their plunder. But they find it difficult to keep peace with one another because they are habituated to making war on mankind. All know that nations are born and die as a result of international battles won and lost. Less noticed but equally true is that any nation defines its character, determines the extent to which it may enjoy internal peace and liberty, by how it deals with matters of war and peace.

Throughout the ages thoughtful persons have noted that while peace among nations does not guarantee peace within each nation, peoples at war with one another do tend to suffer strife among themselves, and that loss of liberty often results even from wars that end in victory. Wars lost or simply long continued produce these tragedies as a matter of course. History teaches us how difficult to gain and easy to lose are domestic harmony and liberty, as well as how dependent they are on peace among nations. In short, peace with "all nations" is a necessary (alas, not a sufficient) condition of "peace among ourselves."

What follows in this book is a history of the ideas concerning the relationship between domestic and international peace that have prevailed in our civilization and especially in our country. This summary of history begins in the Greco-Roman era but moves through time unevenly, slowing down as it approaches our own century, to focus attention on the problems of peace closest to us: Why is *our* America not at peace, its domestic liberty now in danger? What should be our America's peace? What can it be, given our circumstances? How did America's statesmen lose the founding generation's priority for peace? How did they lose sight of the principle that the prospect of peace must rule the conduct of war? How did they come to confuse the very distinction between war and peace, imagining that the American people can live indefinitely without peace?

How did our national-security state arise? What can we expect from it?

Peace and Civilization in the West

Thucydides's history of the Peloponnesian War is written as a tragedy: As the Greek cities of the fifth century BC fought one another, they undermined civilization within themselves. Thucydides begins with an account of how Greek civilization was born out of the legendary king Minos's establishment of peace in the Aegean world, describes its flowering, and then contrasts the wonders of Periclean Athens born of peace with the hell-on-earth of the revolution that resulted from war throughout Greece. For two and a half millennia, that history had cautioned readers.

America's founders took particular note of how the Athenian people had thrown away their precious democracy under the lash of war. The founders also looked upon Rome's greatness as tragedy of a different sort. Rome, history's greatest winner of wars, had shown that when human qualities such as valor, virtue, inventiveness, and dedication, admirable though they be, are used to dominate foreigners they produce all-consuming strife and oppression at home.

Christianity had biased medieval civilization's mind toward peace. Jesus's distinction of duties to God and to Caesar, as well as His dedication of mankind to a kingdom "not of this world," taught classical civilization's Christian heirs that spiritual concerns take precedence over worldly ones. The Hebrew Bible's account of God as Father of all mankind gave Christians further reason to resist lending themselves to war, and fit well with Greek philosophy's discovery of a single human nature naturally ordained to intellection. The cause of peace also benefited politically from the fact that the Germanic tribes who inherited temporal power over Roman lands limited each other's pretensions by guarding their individual independence. But translating preference for peace into practice has been the ever-difficult work of millennia.

Christians assert that since government exists to serve the people's secular interest, the primordial of which is peace, war can only be a means to establish peace or an extraordinary counter to threats to peace. Moreover, because peace is everybody's interest, war cannot be merely the business of sovereigns.

Sovereignty itself is problematic for Christians. Saints Augustine and Aquinas, having distinguished power from truth, warned that claiming sovereignty over both violates man's divinely ordained nature, and hazards peace as well. Nevertheless, Europe's kings and clergy indulged humanity's innate thirst for all manner of power and deference. Only gradually did Christianity's ethos of peace and freedom become part of Western statesmanship—first and partially in England, then to flower in America's English colonies.

In England, the imported Germanic feudal tradition was responsible at least as much as Christian theology for lords' and then for commons' imposition of the Magna Carta of 1215, and then of financial restrictions on kings' power to make war. The ensuing complexity of the English regime's roots underlined the appropriateness of Sir John Fortescue's fifteenth-century description of it as *dominium politicum et regale,* in which king and country must collaborate for the common good. Attachment to this medieval vision animated resistance to the royal absolutism of the fifteenth through eighteenth centuries. The resisters' party, called Whigs, was the trunk out of which America's English revolutionaries branched.

We see the Whig trunk's character most clearly in the writings of Henry St. John Viscount Bolingbroke—a Tory—who, in the early eighteenth century, defined the "loyal opposition" to the king's court by what he called "the country party." Bolingbroke wrote against Machiavelli's exclusion of natural right from public life, and in opposition to unnecessary war. Machiavelli had eclipsed the distinction between right and wrong by assuming the normalcy of war. Bolingbroke was neither the first nor last to note that war empowers royal absolutism.

America, Founded for Peace

America's settlers had not crossed the Atlantic to fight battles of their own, much less the king's. The New England colonies took enthusiastic part in war against France's Quebec primarily to secure their frontier against the horrific Indian raids that the French were sponsoring. But by the mid-eighteenth century the British habit of trying to command colonial militias for imperial priorities rather than for domestic peacekeeping had worn thin the colonists' loyalties. After the French and Indian War of 1763 had ended these raids, participation in the British Empire became synonymous to Americans with domestic oppression.

Thenceforth, the Americans' supreme request of British authorities was to be left in peace. In 1774 Thomas Jefferson, echoing countless preachers and local authorities, described the "rights of British America" in terms of the people's natural right to have, to hold, and to dispose of lives and property, a right that comes from God and hard work (cf. John Locke) rather than from any potentate. The Americans of 1776–83 fought to be equals among the nations of the earth, from which they hoped only mutual forbearance.

Historically literate and conscious that their physically enormous country and fast-growing population guaranteed some kind of greatness, the Americans rejected Rome's kind of greatness because Rome's conquests abroad had produced bloody corruption and despotism at home. Americans, who were eager to show the stars and stripes "at Canton, in the Indus and Ganges," also tried to limit their international intercourse to commercial reciprocity—*vide* John

Adams's unsuccessful 1776 design of a purely commercial "model" for future treaties.

But the Revolutionary War reminded the founding generation of statesmanship's timeless fundamental: *si vis pacem para bellum*. If you want peace, ready yourself for war. Thus Alexander Hamilton and James Madison condensed the lessons of international reality into George Washington's 1796 Farewell Address: "Observe good faith and justice towards all nations; cultivate peace and harmony with all." From that followed Washington's "great rule": "in extending our commercial relations to have with them as little political connection as possible . . . even our Commercial policy should hold an equal and impartial hand: neither seeking nor granting exclusive favours or preferences; consulting the natural course of things; diffusing & deversifying by gentle means the streams of Commerce, but forcing nothing."[1]

Americans might enter into offensive or defensive alliances in extraordinary circumstances, such as the Revolution. But ordinarily, said Washington, Americans ought to refrain from espousing or opposing foreign causes. Rather, they ought to build the power to pursue their own.

Washington was emphatic about this because the mere possibility of American involvement in the wars of the French Revolution had come close to ripping apart the young nation's body politic. These conflicts would lead the administration of President John Adams to try forcibly securing domestic peace by that era's version of "homeland security"—the 1798 Alien and Sedition Acts. But that historically literate generation remembered that the inherent futility of such measures was well known even to Machiavelli. Domestic strife subsided only two years later, when Adams's combination of naval power and diplomacy ended America's "quasi-war" with France.

The sixteen years of Thomas Jefferson and James Madison's presidencies were plagued and well-nigh defined by inability to deal with foreign war's powerfully divisive influence at home. Both presidents tried to keep out of the Napoleonic wars by balancing increasingly warring factions at home, and by mere economic sanctions abroad. But, they ended up having to fight the War of 1812—a war as disastrous at home as it was abroad—because they had stopped building the navy that Washington and Adams had started, and unarmed diplomacy proved impotent to diminish British and French pressure on America. New England almost seceded from the Union, the British Army burned Washington, DC, and Britain's Indian allies massacred the first settlement of Chicago.

Priorities

It was left to John Quincy Adams, whose career began under Washington and ended during the Mexican War of 1848, to define and engineer national consensus on a foreign policy of peace commensurate with America's character. Adams worked under the gathering clouds that would unleash civil war, a catastrophe from which few nations ever recover.

For Adams, the purpose of foreign policy was to preserve a nation defined by the Declaration of Independence, "a beacon on the summit of the mountain to which all the inhabitants of the earth may turn their eyes . . . a light of admonition to the rulers of men, a light of salvation and redemption to the oppressed."[2] It was to be preserved by recognizing that "the first and paramount duty of the government is to maintain peace amidst all the convulsions of foreign wars, and to enter the lists as parties to no cause, other than our own." That meant that while America had no interest in quarrels purely European, it did have an irreducible interest in wars at sea, "the common possession of mankind." America's interest in lands on our borders and islands nearby is next to that of our own internal affairs.

To assert those interests, Adams counseled forswearing involvement in faraway quarrels while warning the world that America would mind the business that it considers its own. That is because, said Adams, "She well knows that by once enlisting under banners other than her own . . . she would involve herself beyond the power of extrication, in all the wars of interest and intrigue, of avarice envy, and ambition, which assume the colors and usurp the standard of freedom." America's glory, unlike Rome's, is to be liberty, not dominion. "She has a spear and a shield: but the motto upon her shield is Freedom, Independence, Peace."[3]

Adams's paradigm for peace meant tailoring the ends of foreign policy to the Declaration of Independence, and then calibrating those ends to the means available.

What was to be America's peace was high among the antebellum generation's controversies. For some, notably Stephen Douglas, the most prominent Democrat of the age, growing America to maximum size and power was important enough to transcend concerns about the ethos of the states that would come into the Union from former Mexican territories and perhaps Latin America. Whigs who followed Adams argued that such nonchalance risked both America's character and its internal peace. Abraham Lincoln made that point in 1846 in opposition to the Mexican War, as well as in his 1858 debates with Douglas.

The division cut across partisan and sectional lines, however. Although most Southern Democrats were eager to add new slave-holding states, forcefully if need be, others, like Georgia's Alexander Stephens, argued that expansion abroad by war meant degeneracy at home. Conversely, not a few prominent Northern Whigs believed that governing Latin Americans without their consent would bring liberty, peace, and progress to the entire hemisphere—counting neither whether this was compatible with America's character nor with its means. In short, questions about what is to be America's peace transcended the issues of the Civil War.

A Taste for More

That war stimulated the winners' sense that they had the capacity, right, and duty radically to improve mankind—a sense in which the losers joined within a generation. This sense was contrary to how Lincoln had approached "peace among ourselves and with all nations." Already in 1838 Lincoln had prescribed reverential adherence to law's restraints as the remedy for domestic strife. In 1861 he sought to pull the nation from the brink of war by promising no interference whatever in the domestic affairs of the Southern states. After the South started shooting, he sought militarily to shorten the war and to return to the status quo ante. Lincoln undertook emancipation of slaves as a necessary war measure. The end in sight, he bid the nation make no distinction between winners and losers, ascribing responsibility to all for the suffering of all, and bidding all to "bind up the nation's wounds" and to take care of its widows and orphans.

For Lincoln, ending the war required restoring domestic harmony, the very contrary of what resulted from the "nation-building" that the radical Republicans imposed on the South after Lincoln's death until 1877—violent, impotent, but pregnant with lasting strife.

The secretaries of state who set the tone for American foreign policy during the nineteenth century's last third, William Seward and James G. Blaine, were indebted intellectually to John Quincy Adams and did their best to follow his paradigm of peace at home and abroad. But the literature of that "gilded age" reflected a mood ebullient with the craving to make very big improvements at home and in the world, coupled with careless confidence about how trying to reform mankind would affect the peace that all wanted. The most popular book of the age, Josiah Strong's *Our Country: Its Possible Future and Its Present Crisis* (1885), celebrated the growing American giant as God's, and Charles Darwin's, designee for global improvement and domination—to be achieved without firing a shot. The same year, Princeton professor Woodrow Wilson's *Congressional Government: A Study in American Politics* decried the US constitutional system's constraints on presidential power to pursue progress. Alfred Thayer Mahan's *The Influence of Sea Power upon History* (1890) invited Americans to think of themselves as successors to Britain's role in the world.

Hence while America's opinion-makers were not bellicose, they had come to believe that they, even more than their European counterparts, were duty bound to "take up the white man's burden"—as Rudyard Kipling put it.

Cuba's 1896–98 revolt against Spanish rule, "right on our doorstep," proved to be an irresistible temptation to do good by force of arms. That and the conquest of the Spanish empire in the Philippines and the Caribbean, almost as an afterthought, gave rise to a brief burst of outright imperialist sentiment. Senator Albert Beveridge of Indiana, its foremost exponent, said that while America's first century had been about governing itself, its second century would be about governing others—a forthright repudiation of the Declaration of Independence. But that forthrightness, coupled with the human cost of governing the Filipinos without their consent, recalled American opinion to its republican fundamentals.

This, however, uncovered a division that had been growing among imperialism's supporters and opponents. Some redoubled their long-standing opposition to military expenditures and force in general, even while continuing to promote commitments abroad—for example, Woodrow Wilson. Others, traditional advocates of military power, stressed the need to match commitments with military capacity, even while cooling on commitments—for example, Theodore Roosevelt.

Ends vs. Means

Thus as the twentieth century began so did a polarization that continues into our own between those who maintain that America must secure its peace by balancing commitments with military capacity, prioritizing them according to what is nearest and dearest, and others who see it dependent on improving mankind regardless of what that might take.

The latter logic culminated in President George W. Bush's Second Inaugural Address's statement that "The survival of liberty in our land increasingly depends on the success of liberty in other lands. The best hope for peace in our world is the expansion of freedom in all the world." No more than his predecessors did Bush explain how to make that happen. Rather, following the hundred-year-old lead of Republican Elihu Root and of Democrat Woodrow Wilson, Bush assumed that the world is longing for freedom as America understands it, and that America need but put itself on the side of peace and progress. By that logic, as much at the turn of the twenty-first century as at the turn of the twentieth, commitment to mankind without end or reckoning of cost trumps America's interest in its own peace.

Woodrow Wilson's pitch to Americans to enter the Great War in 1917, and two years later to join the League of Nations, was based on the assumption of a world moving inexorably to peaceful, democratic freedom, a world that longed for America to join it in overcoming the last remaining obstacles. But reality was that the Great War's belligerents were interested in aggrandizement, and later in revenge and security. That war brought the American people domestic strife such as it had not experienced since the Civil War, in addition to deaths at the front and from the flu of 1918. The disconnect between the words by which Wilson had gained America's support for war and the realities thereof convinced the public that statesmanship itself is fraud. It engendered a pacifism as pervasive as it was mindless.

Wilson and his followers, far from admitting their misunderstanding of reality, insisted that a world safe for democracy really would have come about if only their domestic political opponents had not questioned his idealism, thus preemptively blaming them for whatever might befall mankind. Wilsonians held Republicans in general and Wilson's chief antagonist, Senator Henry Cabot Lodge in particular, responsible for World War II. Hollywood even produced a 1944 movie to this effect, featuring Cedric Hardwicke as the villainous Lodge.

Pacifism, War, and Division

The history of the twentieth century's Interwar period well nigh defines the fact that pacifism is the enemy of peace, domestic as well as international. While the American people high and low had sworn off military commitments, elites of both parties had redoubled their preexisting consensus that America should lead the world to peace and freedom—if not by force then by bribery and exhortation. This bipartisan consensus had given up on the means but retained the ends of global reform.

The Washington naval arms control treaty of 1921 and the contemporaneous nine-power treaty on China illustrate the consequences of committing to grandiose ends while forswearing the means of effecting them. Republican Secretary of State Charles Evans Hughes drew near-universal praise for brokering agreements by nine nations (but principally America and Japan) to respect China's sovereignty, in exchange for America depriving itself of the military capacity to make anyone respect that promise. This amounted to what Theodore Roosevelt had called combining "the unbridled tongue with the unready hand."[4]

When Japan set about conquering China in 1931, Presidents Herbert Hoover and Franklin Roosevelt spent the subsequent decade hectoring Japan while doing nothing to protect China; foreclosing the possibility of peace, yet unwilling to prepare for the war they were making inevitable. Thus did they encourage Americans to outdo one another for political advantage by speaking loudly while whittling away America's sticks. These presidents shared public opinion's pacifism, feared offending it, and continued to feed its illusions.

No illusions were greater nor proved more fateful than those about the Soviet Union. George Washington, scarred as he had been by the conflict between American supporters and opponents of the French Revolution, had warned Americans against "inordinate affection" for another country. But some twentieth-century Americans' affection for the Soviet Union and communism far exceeded that of eighteenth-century Jeffersonians for France. Affection for the Soviet Union and communism deformed US foreign policy, caused World War II to end not in peace but in Cold War, and occasioned conflict among Americans the consequences of which are with us yet.

The promise of permanent, universal peace was a key part of the Soviet Union and communism's lure. It fit all too well with American Progressives' penchant for imagining themselves stewards of mankind rather than mere fiduciary agents of ordinary Americans. Stalin's promise of a benevolent, progressive, Soviet-American co-domination of the planet seduced a class of influential Americans into identifying themselves with that vision—and with him.

The class affected by that vision and affection, a mixture of gentry and intellectuals, was part of the Democratic Party coalition that virtually monopolized power in America between 1932 and 1946. Such stalwarts of the Roosevelt administration as Harry Hopkins (who acted as deputy president throughout the war) and Alger Hiss (who counseled the dying Roosevelt at the 1945 Yalta conference that set the stage for the Cold War) mixed commitment to the Soviet Union with preference for dealing with human affairs in general terms rather than by the jealous squaring of ends and means. Since they believed that Stalin was the sine qua non of perpetual peace through the United Nations, staying on his good side was job #1.

Thus did the Roosevelt administration defer defining America's concrete, particular objectives for peace in favor of propitiating Stalin; it refused to soil its hands with the messy details of peacemaking until events had largely tied America's.

As the advent of Cold War proved their vision of peace false to reality, this vision and its sponsors came under heavy criticism, including from elements of Roosevelt's own coalition. But Roosevelt's class, much as their Wilsonian predecessors had done, blamed their fellow Americans as troglodytes at best and at worst as enemies of all good things. The resulting exacerbation of preexisting domestic sociopolitical divisions has been a key element of America's growing partisan strife into our time.

Our statesmen dealt with their failure to deliver real peace by trying to shift responsibility to the United Nations. Although the UN was never about peace nor embodied any consensus among the world's peoples, our statesmen parried questions about the wisdom of their actions by arguing that their adherence to the UN placed them beyond discussion. By thus pretending to shift responsibility, they asserted the right to make war or peace as they please regardless of the US body politic—a tactic that the administrations of Presidents Clinton, both Bushes, and Obama have practiced in our time.

During World War II the Wilsonian practice of substituting meaningless generalities for the active verbs and proper nouns of dictionaries and grammar books engendered a code by which politicians shield their reasoning about war and peace from the judgment of mere citizens. Alas, not having to explain to fellow citizens what they intend frees them from explaining it fully to themselves.

The Cold War Establishment

Fighting World War II with only generalities (often contradictory) as guidance about the peace to be sought, countless military and civilian officials had thus become habituated to improvising objectives for the power they were wielding. During the Cold War that followed, American statesmen from John Foster Dulles in the 1950s to Henry Kissinger in the 1970s continued to make policy in terms of contradictory generalities, combining theoretical pursuit of the phantom objective of universal peace with nonchalance about how to achieve it. They increasingly confused America's peace with the continuation of that very same Cold War.

No surprise then that America's burgeoning military-civilian national security establishment took on the attributes of a class ever more absorbed in its own internal interests.

An increasingly powerful bipartisan ruling class accustomed to confusing peace and war, and a population habituated to accept lack of peace as normalcy, may well have been the Cold War's deadliest legacy. Dismissal of rational argument, of historical experience and priorities on the ground that they don't apply to an age of radical novelty was no less a lasting and pernicious legacy of that era.

The notion that the Cold War consisted of an American commitment to "contain" the Soviet Union, pursued consistently from circa 1947 to the Soviet collapse of 1991 could not be farther from reality. In fact, "containment" was a compromise between one minority of Americans intent on pursuing peace by cooperating with the Communist world's expansion, and another that sought peace by rolling it back. Over the ensuing half century that compromise unraveled as the two sides drew from the middle and the chasm between them deepened. The longer the Cold War lasted, the more it heated political strife among Americans.

At every stage, American Cold War policy matched the character of domestic politics. From the late 1940s through the 1950s the domestic consensus fit well with George F. Kennan's recommendation of 1947, that resisting communism's threats and blandishments would require Americans above all to reaffirm and reinforce their commitment to their own identity. America's faithfulness to itself would help lead the community of nations to exclude the Soviets. These years were characterized by President Dwight Eisenhower's advice that Americans go to church, by the Boy Scouts, and by books such as Will Herberg's *Protestant-Catholic-Jew: An Essay in American Religious Sociology* (1956), which celebrated America's social conservatism.

The Ruling Class Turns

By the 1970s the Cold War had contributed to deep changes in American public life. Much of what had seemed right about America since its founding now seemed wrong. The Supreme Court had outlawed prayer in the public schools and was pushing religion out of the public square. Desecrating the American flag was now a constitutional right, as was abortion. Government in America was growing at all levels, and the Cold War was starting to habituate citizens to regard all officials with some of the authority due to those who direct military operations. Officials who had regarded themselves as servants merely representing a rightly sovereign people were habituating themselves to act as entitled to rule by virtue of expertise and ideology.

A similar reversal occurred regarding national security. By the mid-1970s bipartisan experts had formed a new consensus that the United States should work and hazard much to bring the Soviet Union into the community of nations, and even to facilitate its hold on its empire. By that logic, Americans whose view of the Cold War was "we win, they lose" (as Ronald Reagan encapsulated it) were illegitimate.

Reagan's 1980s were a partial respite in these changes' progress. But their international and domestic elements quickly resumed their advance, regardless even of the Soviet Union's demise and the Cold War's end.

Logic played little part in the elite consensus's development. One reason is the unreason associated with nuclear weapons. Its essence, contained in Bernard Brodie's *The Absolute Weapon: Atomic Power and World Order* (1946), is that nuclear weapons guarantee that war means mutual annihilation. It was summarized most succinctly in songster Tom Lehrer's "we will all go together when we go" (1959). Its practical lesson was illustrated by the movie "On the Beach" (1959): in the face of death, nothing makes any difference.

Acceptance of this dogma absolves statesmen of the responsibility to consider the precise effect of their actions. Following that mentality, three generations of our ruling class have refused to build anti-missile defenses for America, despite the public's steadfast belief that they should and actually do exist. Three score and ten years during which we have had neither peace nor annihilation have not shaken that dogma's hold.

The bipartisan ruling class that grew in the Cold War, who imagined themselves and who managed to be regarded as entitled by expertise to conduct America's business of war and peace, protected its status against a public from which it continued to diverge by translating the commonsense business of war and peace into a private, pseudo-technical language impenetrable to the uninitiated. Its paradigm, Thomas Schelling's *The Strategy of Conflict* (1960), assumes pseudo-scientifically that international affairs are contests between interchangeable units within an inescapable matrix of choices. Henry Kissinger, who translated that pretense into English in *Nuclear Weapons and Foreign Policy* (1957) and *The Necessity for Choice: Prospects of American Foreign Policy* (1961), was foremost among supposed experts who have been intellectually responsible for America's national security for a half-century.

The commonplace that the Cold War shifted power over peace and war from the legislative to the executive branch overshadows the underlying fact that power went not so much from one set of the American people's representatives to another, but rather from elected officials to professionals not responsible to the voters. Elected officials and "experts" formed a ruling class with its own particular mentality.

Its "school solution" to ominous events abroad has been and continues to be to "do something," because "doing nothing" would be dangerous. But then, because they deem defeating the enemy (perhaps, even, identifying the enemy) to be even more dangerous than "doing nothing," they decide to send Americans to kill and die without a plan for peace. Moreover, they do their best to minimize the American people's involvement, believing that questions of war and peace are beyond the American people's simplemindedness.

But that class's stewardship has brought us no victories, no peace; instead we have had war with foreigners and strife among ourselves. American troops are sent. They win the battles. American policy loses the war. Domestic strife increases another notch. America loses more respect and gains more enemies. The cycle repeats.

Half Commitment and Consequence

The unraveling compromise at the heart of US "containment" policy and fear of nuclear apocalypse combined to produce a yet unbroken series of no-win wars. It began in Korea, 1950. Having conceded China and the northern half of Korea to the then-united Communist empire, our ruling class seemed ready to concede Korea's southern half as well, until the Communist powers invaded it. Having then decided somehow that "containment" must apply to South Korea, our ruling class fumbled fatefully.

Containment's logic called for responding to the empire's attempted "breakouts" so as to discourage further attempts. That required inflicting a net loss to the empire's integrity. But our ruling class decided not to inflict that loss, rather to suffer the loss of over fifty thousand American lives to produce an outcome that divided Americans. This invited our enemies to repeat the exercise.

They did that in Vietnam. When the Soviet Union (and to a lesser extent China) supplied and directed North Vietnam's attack on its Western-allied neighbor, our ruling class chose yes, to respond, but no, not to inflict any penalty on any part of the Communist empire (then on the way of dissolution) or even to cut off the invasion's supply lines by sea and rail. The US Vietnam War consisted of gradually feeding more and more troops to the front. But the Communists had learned that the amount of US manpower does not matter, so long as the Americans remain wedded to their habit of fighting without a serious plan for defeating or destroying the enemy.

The problem with that is straightforward: If you don't have a reasonable plan for winning your peace, your level of effort is irrelevant.

America's defeat in Vietnam was systemic. While US military operations were merely wasteful, the operations of America's ruling class proceeded from intellectual corruption and produced a social revolution at home. Who was the enemy in Vietnam and what was to be done about that enemy? President Lyndon Johnson refrained from pointing to the North Vietnamese politburo—never mind to the Soviet and Chinese ones. Rather, he indicted "poverty, ignorance, and disease." Accordingly, US strategy in Vietnam consisted of socio-economic-political "nation-building" supposedly shielded by military operations.

global meliorism

That recipe for disaster remains the US government's default approach.

Meanwhile significant parts of the ruling class, led by such officials as Secretary of Defense Robert McNamara, identified the enemy as conservative Americans who, like Barry Goldwater, wanted to fight the war to victory or not fight it at all. These domestic enemies, McNamara wrote, were a danger to peace greater than the Communist powers. Laying the blame for the Vietnam War on domestic conservatives proved to be more consequential than anything that happened on the battlefields.

Although "learning the lessons of Vietnam" became something of a literary and bureaucratic industry, our ruling class has never ceased to follow the pattern established in Korea and Vietnam: regardless of the amount of force deployed, the US government does not identify the enemy whose elimination would produce our peace. Thus instead of eliminating obstacles to peace, it creates new ones. The Gulf War of 1990 was paradigmatic. A half-million superbly equipped US troops destroyed Iraq's invasion force in Kuwait. The US government assumption was that this would shield a vast socio-economic-political "peace process" in the Middle East. But, once again, US policy had avoided choosing between not intervening in a foreign war and eliminating an enemy so as to discourage others.

Counter to Machiavelli's proverbial advice never to do an enemy a little harm, the US government left a wounded Saddam Hussein in power in Iraq, and stationed troops in Saudi Arabia indefinitely to "keep him in a box." Earlier, troops had been stationed throughout the Persian Gulf in the aftermath of Iran's seizure of the US Embassy in Tehran, in lieu of having responded with war to this act of war. It should have surprised no one that using military power indecisively and stationing troops in alien lands generate contempt for and violence against America.

President George H. W. Bush's justification for the Gulf War of 1990—building "a new world order"—illustrates why the Soviet Union's demise did not usher in an era of peace for America. The American people's wholehearted, visceral rejection of imperialism notwithstanding, our ruling class imagines itself endowed and

Crichton's of fear
State

obliged to superintend such an order. Wars, terrorism, and "homeland security" projected out to eternity have followed inexorably.

Engagement and Identity

In the post-Cold War environment of reduced risk, the inertial force of habits acquired over three generations kicked in and led our ruling class to ever-deeper involvement in more countries, with less and less force relative to the problems at hand, with less and less calculation of ends and means, much less of care for the American people's peace. Neither waging war in the dictionary meaning of the term nor giving to other peoples the peace that Americans expect from them, our ruling class justified foreign engagements to itself in terms of its own components' ideologies: liberal internationalism, neoconservatism, and realism.

These variants of turn-of-the-twentieth-century progressivism have more in common than not. All regard foreigners as yearning for American leadership. Their proponents regard foreigners as mirror images of themselves, at least potentially. Liberal internationalists see yearners for secular, technocratic development. Neoconservatives see budding democrats, while realists imagine peoples inclined to moderation. Hence the establishment's various sectors struggle over "development aid," "democracy promotion," and the search for "moderates" by expressing often-contradictory recipes in fuzzy language. It is seldom clear, even to the advocates of "engagement" or of "assistance" or of "bombing," why these means should produce the results they expect—just what *this* alignment with a foreign faction, *those* subsidies, the destruction of *these* bombing targets, the killing of *those* individuals, or what those "boots on the ground" (boots?) would do to secure America's peace.

Different emphases notwithstanding, there is solid consensus among our ruling-class factions that America's great power requires exercising responsibility for acting as the globe's "policeman," sheriff, "umpire," "guardian of international standards," "stabilizer," or "leader"—whatever one may call it. If America shuns that responsibility, the world will slide into chaos, and America will lose the peace. Just as broad and solid as in the Interwar Years, however, is the consensus that America will not do whatever it takes effectively to police, or sheriff, or guard, or somehow to lead, because such things take an awful bloody lot of doing.

Hence the American ruling class's consensus that it has the right and duty to prod if not to shove foreigners up the evolutionary ladder, its coupling of grandiose ends with squeamishness about means, guar- _—Cp. 11-12_ antees unending conflict with all nations and strife among ourselves.

Few pay attention to the main issue of foreign policy: its effect on America's own character. America's own soul is the ultimate stake. That peculiar, exceptional soul is the source of America's external power and above all of its internal peace.   _exceptionalism_

The ruling-class consensus that many, prolonged, inconclusive involvements all over the world are a permanent, sustainable feature of America's life is wrong, because these lead America to forget what it is about. Such involvements abet that forgetting precisely as John Quincy Adams had said: Because these are "wars of interest and intrigue, of avarice envy, and ambition, which assume the colors and usurp the standard of freedom." Affirming our own justice is impossible precisely because the killing and dying in such struggles is on behalf of others' "interest and intrigue, of avarice envy, and ambition" rather than about ourselves, and because the outcomes are not under our control.

Specifically, when we kill and die in struggles between foreign sects or ethnicities, or political factions, we cannot help but be agnostic about what the warring parties care for most deeply. The necessity of working intimately with some and against others compels us to tolerate a host of alien ways. Thus trained to find direction with others' compasses, we lose faith in our own. Our ruling class, having set aside America's standards about what is worthy of toleration and what not, came to tolerate its foreign counterparts and acquired the habit of stigmatizing its own American competitors as intolerable. Peace at home became as problematic as peace abroad.

No-Win Wars Come Home

Beginning in the mid-1960s, the US government treated the hijacking of airplanes and ships, the bombings and mass shootings at airports and at the Olympics, the murder of its ambassadors as minor irritations. The Nixon administration's main response was to ban Americans from carrying guns on airplanes. Thus practically it absolved the governments that sheltered the hijackers from responsibility and sent a fateful message.

In 1979, when Iran's revolutionary government seized the US embassy and its diplomats, and our bipartisan ruling class (both the Carter and Reagan administrations) did not treat it as the textbook *casus belli* that it was, the complex of foreign and domestic war that afflicts twenty-first-century Americans came of age. The Islamic world learned that it was now safe to export its warfare to the West in general and to America in particular.

The American ruling class's response would continue along its twin rails: no-win wars, and "homeland security."

Since 9/11, our politicians and academics, the media and the entertainment industry have flooded the country with explanations, justifications, and recipes about "the war." But nothing in this flood is about how peace may be established or how the freedoms that characterized American life may be restored. Rather, the focus of discourse has been on our warfare's inevitability and on the need for Americans to submit to a new way of life, forever.

This mentality is rooted in misunderstanding of the Muslim world and of America itself.

Willfully ignorant of all religion, our ruling class took for granted that Islam was even more a relic of the past than Christianity. It failed to see that Islam and its law were reasserting themselves in Persian Iran, the Arab Middle East, and the rest of the Muslim world roughly in proportion to Western civilization's evident weakening and to the failure of their westernizing regimes to embody appealing cultural models. It did not grasp that the Ayatollah Khomeini's 1979 overthrow of Iran's Shah signified that a whole civilization was being mobilized against America, and that this is a big, multidimensional problem. Nor did it see beyond the cynicism of such secularists as Saddam Hussein who styled themselves as champions of Islam, thus helping to redefine Islam in anti-Western terms. Nor did it grasp that Islam's perennial internal struggles are being won by its most violent elements—the Wahabis and the Muslim Brotherhood.

Instead, the judgment that flowed from the CIA through the George W. Bush White House to the media and hence into America's capillaries was that 9/11, and by implication the rest of terrorism, was the doing of Osama bin Laden's al-Qaeda. The notion that this, *or any set of "rogues,"* is the proximate (never mind the ultimate) cause of anti-American terrorism was always patent nonsense.

Al-Qaeda was a set of some two hundred men, mostly Arabs, who had joined bin Laden in Afghanistan to fight the Soviet invasion and had stayed. Imputing responsibility to these "Afghan Arabs," *persons extraneous to the Muslim world's ruling class* with which the US government has what it considers good relations, delimited what US policymakers considered to be the problem. Conveniently, this diverted attention from weighty religious-cultural factors.

But tailoring US actions to that narrowly defined problem guaranteed that no amount of effort would bring peace.

Overthrowing Afghanistan's Taliban regime and killing or jailing most of the "Afghan Arabs" in 9/11's immediate aftermath showed that our ruling class had not thought of how to secure peace. No one contended that overthrowing the Taliban had vanquished or significantly diminished terrorism. Yet had President George W. Bush taken seriously his own vow of September 20, 2001, to make no distinction between terrorists and those who harbor them, he could have used the Taliban's overthrow to demand of any number of Muslim countries that they turn over any number of terrorists to America or face the same fate. Instead, the US government began to apply to Afghanistan its default "nation-building" recipe: strengthening the central government vis-à-vis the provinces, though this meant disarming the very tribes that had helped win the victory against the Taliban; and spreading civilian advisers throughout the land bearing inflammatory advice on how to live.

The US government also decided to overthrow Saddam Hussein's regime in Iraq. But why? By logic, defining military operations follows tightly from defining the ends that the operations are to serve. By nature, this work of definition consists of the deliberative concatenation of ends and means. This requires asking: What is the problem? Will these operations' success restore the peace? The test of military operations is whether, if and when they are successful at killing the people intended to be killed, the troubles persist or not. Our ruling class did not ask those questions. Nor did it use Saddam's overthrow as a warning to anti-American rulers in the region. Instead, it applied to Iraq as well its default remedy: socio-economic-political "nation-building" shielded by military forces.

The 2003 invasion of Iraq having overthrown Saddam Hussein, President Bush was strictly correct in stating, aboard the USS *Lincoln,* that America's military "mission" had been "accomplished." But he was disastrously wrong regarding America's peace because the Saudi king, fearing his Persian enemy Iran, along with the US State Department and CIA, had already persuaded him to occupy Iraq indefinitely—that is, to start "Iraq War II." But to do what? Thinly did Bush veil that he never decided.

Each of the Iraq War's combatants—any number of Sunni, Shia, and Kurdish factions, plus their supporters throughout the Muslim world—had coherent, self-interested objectives. The US objective of reducing violence among these combatants was inherently irrelevant to America's peace.

Our ruling class's sense of intellectual-moral entitlement—the very sense by which it bids to reform backward Americans—led it to imagine that the "war on terror" must be pursued by imposing its preferred "human rights" on backward foreigners. In Iraq and Afghanistan, US officials worked hard and alienated many by promoting abortion as well as equal treatment of women. Thus also, every year, all US embassies observe "gay pride month," including rebukes to the locals who dissent from its premises—in the name of the American people. Thus the "war on terror" became a war on peace that further deepened divisions among Americans.

So, internationally, America has less peace than before 9/11. Whereas on the night of that horror governments throughout the Muslim world suppressed anti-American rejoicing out of fear of what America might do, on September 11, 2012, those very governments were neutral or complicit in murderous mob attacks on US embassies in their capitals. The marshaled mobs shouted: "Obama, Obama, there are a billion Osamas." Indeed. America, bloodied and thrashing like a wounded animal, was drawing predators small and large at home as well as abroad.

During the Cold War's early stage America had met a civilizational challenge by strengthening its own civilization. But by the twenty-first century our ruling class, alienated from that civilization and its compass confused by decades of involvement in other nations' quarrels, had doubled down on its Wilsonian sense of intellectual-moral entitlement. It came to regard its domestic political opponents as perhaps the principal set of persons whose backward ways must be guarded against and reformed. Thus did our loss of peace abroad feed domestic strife, and result in the loss of peace at home.

Homeland Security's Systemic Damage

It was to be expected that a ruling class that refuses to pass explicit judgment regarding the international causes and cultures in whose quarrels it partakes would declare itself agnostic about the difference between good citizens and terrorists at home. Our ruling class now acts as though all Americans could be terrorists and it increasingly confuses its own domestic opponents with enemies of the state. It began by demanding that Americans put out of their minds that 9/11 had been perpetrated by Muslims acting on behalf of Muslim causes, that Americans must embrace the counterintuitive proposition that each American is as likely as any other to be a terrorist, and that they trust the government to sift out the terrorists from among us.

Since this sifting is to be part of a struggle against terrorism that is assumed to be synonymous with modernity, that sifting is to be permanent as well. Since 9/11, our ruling class has discouraged, even denigrated, discussion of how the American people's characteristic liberties might be restored. In short, Americans must learn to trust each other less than ever, while trusting the authorities ever more, forever.

The post-9/11 homeland-security state came into being so quickly and smoothly because it fits so well with ruling-class prejudices and interests that had been maturing for generations. 9/11 merely provided impetus and excuse. Whereas Americans used to count the Soviet politburo's use of armored limousines and special traffic lanes as hallmarks of tyranny, our time's hundreds of American VIPs now move with more armed security for themselves and more disruption for others than ever the Politburo did. Whereas in the 1950s cops were few and wore blue, two decades later America was awash in paramilitary SWAT teams. In our time, federal agencies have their own army and conduct military operations against citizens. Whereas in 1963 Alabama Sheriff Bull Connor's use of a mere cattle prod to disperse a crowd scandalized the nation, a generation later the police's use of electroshock "tasers" and pepper spray to convulse (and occasionally kill) individuals who talk back to them had become unremarkable, routine, quotidian. While the courts dally with theories about capital punishment, the nation's many militarized police forces shoot to kill.

In short, the modern homeland-security state is about ever-more control with ever-less explicit discretion. But the homeland-security state is all about increasing its own discretion.

A generation ago, the suggestion that there resides in the executive branch of the US government the right to harm, never mind to kill, an American citizen without due process of law would not have been tolerated. Yet in our time Congress, the Supreme Court, and public opinion seem to have conceded such a right's existence.

In 2010 someone in the Justice Department wrote a document purporting to authorize the nonjudicial killing of a US citizen named Anwar al-Awlaki—the reasoning concerning which, the *New York Times*' report on the document takes pains to assure us, would not apply to any other citizen. But there is nothing in that document— which became official US policy—that might prevent such a death sentence from applying to anyone whom the president and his advisers might designate.

On whom, then, should our security forces focus? In 2013 President Obama said, "We must define the nature and scope of this struggle, or else it will define us. . . ." But neither he nor anyone else in the US government took up that challenge. Yet that power cannot remain unspecified, because apolitical policing of political strife is impossible. It will be used at the discretion and in the interest of the ruling class ad hoc, and will generate corresponding reactions from those it harms.

Human beings naturally crave excuses for treating their political opponents as bad people. What starts as impotent, random harassment ends, as Machiavelli wrote, in the empowerment of the rulers to police for their own ends, and in the alienation of the rest. The American regime is based on recognizing and juxtaposing interests. Barring explicit political decisions from the front door ensures that implicit political decisions flood in through the windows.

And so, our homeland security is politicized. Here, as elsewhere, persons who possess power in government and society have the opportunity to direct blame, distrust, and even mayhem onto those they like least. Since the mid-1990s, authoritative voices from the ruling class have intoned a litany: America is beset by violence from racism, sexism, homophobia, and religious obscurantism, domestic abuse, greed, and the availability of guns. These ills are not so different from those found in backward parts of the world where we fight "extremism" in order to fight terrorism. Indeed, these domestic ills argue for fighting extremism, for nation-building at home as well as abroad. Who in America embodies extremism? Who is inherently responsible for social ills, including terrorism? Who will have to be reconstructed? No surprise: the ruling class's political opponents: the conservative side of American life.

No surprise also that, since 2006, the Department of Homeland Security has used its intelligence "fusion centers" to compile dossiers against such groups as "pro-lifers" and such "anti-government activists" as "homeschoolers" and "gun owners." DHS has its own police force, the Federal Protective Service, and conducts its "practice runs" against mockups of these groups. The Federal Bureau of Investigation for its part infiltrates the Tea Parties as it once did the Communist Party.

None of this domestic partisanship is law, or even official policy, much less conspiracy. Rather, it reflects the prejudices and convenience, the intellectual, social, indeed the very *identity* of those in power. After all, President Barack Obama had called "enemies of democracy" the very groups that the Internal Revenue Service then subjected to punitive audits, and Vice President Joseph Biden had called some of them "terrorists," as has the US Senate's Majority Leader.

Indeed, a Rasmussen poll shows that 26 percent of the Obama administration's supporters—possibly not the least influential among them—regard the Tea Parties as the top terrorist threat to America.

Thus does domestic peace slip away.

Prayer for Peace

How can peace be recovered? How might we go about earning it? The answer lies not in prescriptions of policy but in understanding and practicing fundamentals. The first of these is that America's paramount interest is remaining itself, and hence that the modern American status of confusing peace and war is unnatural and unsustainable both internationally and domestically.

Treating wars as other than temporary struggles to secure our own concrete, vital interests, abandoning the sharp distinction between war and peace, and making commitments without the prospect of peace have brought foreign quarrels to America itself. The homeland security that we are using to deal with these imported troubles does not protect Americans; instead it treats us like foreigners. The government's increased powers offer its many agencies the opportunity to focus their attention on anyone suspected of violating their countless regulations and policies. Homeland security's political correctness grates. Our ruling class's presumption of moral authority to nation-build American society stokes partisan warfare.

Reversing that will require a new generation of statesmen who regard minding America's business—*minding America's peace and winning America's wars* as the American people's fiduciary agents—not as a demotion from the rank of steward of the world but rather as a calling that absorbs the highest human talents. Minding our business is no more the counsel of retreat for us now than it was for Washington, Lincoln, Jefferson, or Theodore Roosevelt: men on Mt. Rushmore.

Such statesmen will not ask foreigners to change their culture, but will demand neither more nor less than peaceful, reciprocal respect. Mindful that peaceably resolving domestic quarrels about what it means to be American is divisive enough without our complicating it with foreign considerations, they will profess and practice neutrality in others' affairs. But, when others trouble America's peace, they will impose that peace by war.

The distinction between "our business" and "their business" is the proximate foundation of peace. The first item of our business is to secure other nations' respect. Guarding respect by making that distinction, by earning a reputation for gravitas, neither giving nor suffering injury or slight, by never doing enemies a little harm while guarding our power to undo them, is our most immediate duty to peace.

The civil war in Syria that began in 2011 provides an object lesson. Havez and Bashar al-Assad regime had been America's enemy from its inception. When this regime was allied with the Soviet Union, when it sponsored the murder of US Marines in Lebanon, or when it acted as headquarters for war against US troops in Iraq, the United States had the capacity to ensure that Assad would be replaced by persons who would trouble our peace less. Hence, undoing him would have been our business. But since Assad's opponents in the civil war of 2011 were just as likely as Assad to trouble America's peace, interfering in that war only meant troubling it further. Hence, what happened between the two sides in that war concerned them, not us.

What, rightly, is our business with foreign despots who do not trouble us? Our founding generation's relationship with Russia— then and often since then the paradigm of tyranny—is exemplar. Secretary of State John Quincy Adams's dealings with Russia aimed to strengthen the peace that existed between the two countries, to state that America would oppose any expansion of Russia's system of government to the Western Hemisphere, as well as to leave no doubt that America was committed to republicanism at least as strongly as the emperor was to monarchy. The peaceful and mutu-ally advantageous relations that followed are a reminder of how different peoples can go about sharing the same planet.

To avoid war, a new generation of American statesmen will heed Theodore Roosevelt's advice to speak words smaller than their sticks; because, when war comes, passions drive violence beyond anyone's control. Mindful that Greek civilization was broken by what started as a small war, that in 1861 neither Union nor Confederacy meant to kill two percent of the United States' population, and that the combatants of 1914 had no idea that they were wrecking European civilization, our new American statesmen will know that there is no such thing as a small war any more than a small pregnancy—that wars are to be avoided or to be won quickly.

Above all, our new statesmen will have been reminded of the timeless truth that "home" is war's most important front, that peace at home is prerequisite for earning peace abroad, and that there is no record of people's mores, institutions, or capacity for domestic peace improving in wartime. They will regard the decision to deal with terrorism through permanent "homeland security" directed against all citizens equally rather than on plausible enemies discriminately as one of history's most fateful errors, an error that gave civil strife's deadly spiral its first deadly turns among us.

Causing that spiral to turn in the direction of peace is a task worthy of prayer.

1

The Nature of Peace

History shows us peace—and the lack thereof—in forms and cir-cumstances always peculiar to time and place, always temporary. Neither mankind nor any part thereof is at peace at all times, any more than it is always at war. Peace is not humanity's default state any more than the opposite. *There is no such thing as peace, simply.* Rather, instances of peace are states of relative satisfaction, states of rest into which some peoples settle after striving against one another. Therefore, we are compelled to ask of any instance of peace: Whose peace is it? Who created it, against whose wishes? Why are some people content to live alongside others in *this* peace? Who upholds it, against what alternative? Conversely, what versions of peace are at stake in any given conflict? The answers fall under the categories of force, interest, and ideas, but always in concrete circumstances and for specific reasons. Hence, the tendency of American statesmen and scholars since the turn of the twentieth century to think of peace in general terms abstracts from reality.

Most often, peace comes when one side succeeds in imposing its version of it upon another—that is, after one side has defeated or exhausted another in war—or when both of war's sides have so exhausted each other that there is no fight left in them. Then the exhausted parties tend to become subjects of others' quarrels and others' versions of peace. The truest of all truths about peace is that *the character of any instance thereof depends on the war that estab-lished it and on the winners' character.*

Peace as Satisfaction

History records the longest periods of peace occurring within great empires at their height. Caesar Augustus had ended Rome's civil wars, had stopped expanding the Roman *limes,* and had devoted the legions to maintaining peace within them—not infrequently by crucifixions. Augustus, not Jesus, was known to contemporaries as the *princeps pacis,* the prince of peace.

Similarly, China's Ming dynasty set aside its Mongol predecessors' expansionism and settled down to rule a peaceful empire. So also the sun never set on the British Empire's nineteenth-century version, maintained by force less exercised than consented to. Much the same can be said of the ancient Persian and other "ecumenical" empires. Such peace partakes of what St. Augustine called *tranquillitas ordinis,* the tranquility of order and of the winners' justice, but seldom of freedom.

Other empires, resulting from other victories, produce a kind of quiet more akin to that found in prisons: the acquiesce of the vanquished, because death is the only alternative. Neither tranquility nor order characterized the empire that resulted from the Soviet Union's victory in World War II. By contrast, the peace that settled on Western Europe after that war is prototypical of those caused by exhaustion, in which quiet is less a sign of order than of necrosis and voluntary subjection. Almost as often, though more briefly, peace comes when former enemies are pushed together by the appearance of enemies common to both. This principle, together with the totality of Imperial Japan's defeat, explains why, after 1950, three generations of peace followed two generations of hostility.

Interest, Honor, and Ideas

Material interests are, if not inherently compatible, then surely inherently adjustable by peaceful means. However, neither compatibility nor adjustability of material interests reliably constitutes a sufficient cause of peace. Were it otherwise, human beings would be far more peaceful than they are. Demonstrating that peace pays better than war has always been as unproblematic as showing that honesty is the best policy.

War, as the German language reminds us, is *kriegen,* or taking. But humanity did not need eighteenth-century economics to discover that the toil and trouble necessary to take from others is greater than what is required to make things for one's self or freely to trade for them. Norman Angell's 1910 *The Great Illusion: A Study of the Relation of Military Power in Nations to Their Economic and Social Advantage* showed without doubt that modern war would destroy far more than any winner might possibly gain from it. Therefore, he concluded, it was impossible. The Socialist movement of that age assured the world that common people had "no fatherland" and hence would not fight wars. Yet in 1914–18 Socialist workers slaughtered one another for their fatherlands' sakes. In our time, the *New York Times'* Thomas Friedman's best selling *The Olive Tree and the Lexus: Understanding Globalization* argues that the Middle East's peoples will stop fighting for their neighbors' olive trees when they realize that peace can let them enjoy the global economy's bounties. They have not done so.

Human beings routinely sweep aside reason about interest. In this regard, today's Middle East is no different from Europe, 1914. Some cultures—Russian and Arab, for example—understand economics itself as exploitation of forcefully established terms of trade, of rent-seeking rather than production. Also, because human beings in general are susceptible to the argument that foreigners are taking unfair advantage of us, Alexander Hamilton's remark in *Federalist* #6 that commercial rivalries and personal factors always have produced, and always will produce, wars, is as valid today as it ever was.

Interest is a shaky basis for peace, because the interest of any people as a whole seldom if ever trumps that of powerful individuals and parties within each. Strife may serve these particular interests better than peace. Again, Hamilton's warning in the same *Federalist* is to the point: "the attachments, enmities, interests, hopes and fears of leading individuals . . . assuming the pretext of some public motive, have not scrupled to sacrifice the national tranquility to personal advantage or personal gratification . . . the influence which the bigotry of one female, the petulancies of another, and the cabals of a third had on the contemporary policy, ferments, and pacifications of a considerable part of Europe are topics that have too often been descanted upon not to be generally known." In short, particular interest trumps general interest, short-term interest trumps long-term interest, and sin often trumps virtue in human affairs.

Heeding the counsel of reason about the country's interest in peace over one's own and one's friends' personal interests and passions takes calculation. But minds controlled by ideas foster peace only to the extent that the ideas being calculated do so. In short, enlightened self-interest requires enlightenment. But oh, the darkness! Our civilization abounds with accounts of ideas and mentalities that utterly exclude peace. Homer's Achilles so embodies the notion of honor that he well-nigh made it impossible to war rationally, much less to imagine peace. (Not so Homer's Odysseus, who longs for family life in his bucolic home.) Roman ideas, *vide* the *Eniad,* are far more about glory than peace.

Closer to our own time, Napoleon showed us how easily glory may warp and wrap a people's mind around wars, precluding thought about wars' end. Marxism-Leninism, its eschatological overlay notwithstanding, was a doctrine of eternal strife for all practical purposes. In this it was indistinguishable from any number of late-medieval Christian heresies, including the ones that animated the crusades as social revolution on the basis of the pretense that "*Deus le veult,*" God wills it. Islam originally and fundamentally divides humanity between *dar al-Islam,* those who have accepted Islam and thus won a claim to living in peace, and those who have not and hence who yet live in "the realm of war," *dar al-harb.* To this realm Muhammad restricted the *ghzaw,* the theretofore-universal Arab practice of killing other tribes' men, raping the women and leaving them to die in the desert. Old Testament Judaism makes a similar distinction, at least as it applies to the Promised Land.

All of the above proceed from the fact that primacy—who kowtows to whom—is more important to human beings than is peace, important enough to kill and die for. That in turn is possible to the extent that one does not conceive of anything that may be done in peace that is more important than mere primacy.

Ideas that value peace do so because they value the things that may be done only in peace, or done best in peace, and conversely that human primacy is not so important. Thus, famously, Socrates forfeited his life, telling the Athenian Assembly: "Men of Athens I love you, but I must obey the god rather than you." Jesus Christ, after telling the Pharisees to "render unto Caesar the things that are Caesar's and unto God the things that are God's," told Pontius Pilate: "My kingdom is not of this world."

Hence for Socrates's and Christ's followers, who rules on earth and to what end is not as important as conforming personal behavior to divine command. Socrates carried his spear in Athens's phalanx, and Christians have fought in their countries' wars. But Platonists and Christians are biased toward peace because they believe that their souls are more important than any war's results. Something similar may be said of Buddhism, which focuses the mind on man's interaction with himself, and with nature. Peaceful, individual cultivation of moral and spiritual virtue trumps the collective pursuit of glory.

Secular humanism is ambivalent about peace. To the extent that ever-more pleasant living is its *summum bonum,* secular humanism is peaceful to the point of pacifism. But secular humanism is also about managing humanity's march toward a higher state of being. That Darwinian march does require at least some violence. Imagining themselves the scientific managers of the planetary ecosystem's evolution, secular humanists see mankind at once as a work-in-progress and as the planet's problem. So, while they view traditional political struggles (abstractly) as less significant than even Christians or Platonists do, in practice they are downright eager to use whatever power may be at hand to trim the planetary garden of humans they judge to be excess or otherwise dysfunctional, to regulate who may eat or otherwise consume what.

Much preferring economic and bureaucratic regulation to naked force, secular humanists are nevertheless not averse to using force to suppress resistance to progress, that is, to themselves. Secular humanism's peace, then, is less a choice to forego strife for the sake of higher concerns than it is the rulers' satiation and the peace of the prison for the rest.

2

Peace, Civilization, and War

Because war's passions raise stakes to inherently uncontrollable heights, regimes that engage in war, no matter how small the war may be at first, thereby place their own lives—and the life of civilization itself—in the balance. Because all manner of civilization is rooted in peace, no regime, no nation, no civilization is immune from this liability. The certainty that departures from peace corrode the place on which statesmen stand makes it incumbent on them constantly to evaluate the gains for which they hope from any given war. They seldom do.

Civilized ways, Thucydides tells us, blossomed in Greece before Homeric times when the legendary king Minos of Crete suppressed the Aegean pirates, at once providing physical safety and delegitimizing life by rapine. The Greeks, no longer having to wonder whether strangers were pirates, moved about more confidently and soon stopped wearing arms. Commerce increased, and manners eased. They invested in the future by building permanent structures, including city walls. Luxury followed peace. Its advent was especially advantageous to the people of Attica. Increased mutual trust made possible the laws of Solon that recognized neighbors as fellow Athenians. Until after the Persian wars, Athens and similar cities maintained peace by moderating their quarrels.

Sparta was rooted in a very different type of peace. The *Spartiates* conquered the Helot tribes of the Peloponnesus, made them into slaves who fulfilled all economic functions, and devoted themselves to maintaining military mastery over them. Whenever a new Spartan king took office, he would re-declare war on the Helots.

Sparta never built walls because the *Spartiates* were full-time professional warriors, in arms at all times. Sparta's was the peace of an armed camp. The *Spartiates* too moderated their quarrels with neighbors, but that was because they had to stay close to home lest the Helots rebel. Fear of a slave revolt also made this warrior class averse to hazarding serious losses and hence biased toward international peace.

Whatever the source of moderation, the roughly three centuries that preceded the Persian wars of 480–470 BC produced a civilization of widespread wealth, attachment to law, and unprecedented intellectual sophistication. Thus, the Greeks' distinction between themselves and those they termed "barbarians," of whom Aristotle wrote that they could be ruled only by tyrants, was objective, factual. Just as factual was the destruction of that civilization by the loss of peace.

The Fall of Greece

By the mid-fifth century, Athens had transformed its leadership of Greek seafaring cities into empire over them, and had become dependent on tribute from them for domestic welfare as well as for the splendors still visible today. Sparta worried about Athens's growing greatness, and gave comfort to whatever Greek cities chose to oppose Athens. The great powers' rivalry heightened the normal strife among factions within the smaller cities. In turn, these rivalries fired the fears and ambitions of the great powers' leading personages. Thus, what had begun as a contest between Athens and Sparta for leadership in keeping the Persian Empire at bay eventuated into the Peloponnesian War, a war that became an end in itself, ended up destroying the Greek world's peace, undermined its civilization, and erased the very distinction between Greeks and barbarians.

Arguably Thucydides's most poignant lesson is that none of the war's participants, especially in Athens, were moved by any notion of the peace that might result from their sacrifices.

Thucydides's account of Pericles's funeral speech sums up what peace had meant to Greeks who had learned from Athens, "the school of Hellas":

The freedom we enjoy in our government extends also to our ordinary life . . . all this ease in our private relations does not make us lawless as citizens . . . our chief safeguard . . . that code which although unwritten yet cannot be broken without acknowledged disgrace . . . where our rivals from their very cradles by a painful discipline seek after manliness, we live exactly as we please, and yet are just as ready to encounter every legitimate danger . . . we cultivate refinement without extravagance and knowledge without effeminacy. . . ."[1]

In short, Athenian civilization had achieved a happy balance between opposing human qualities: self-seeking and public spiritedness, duty and pleasure. But war upset that balance. It usually does.

Growing, all-consuming ferocity did the upsetting by leading men to think more of the struggle itself than of what might come of it. Within Athens itself, partisan passions made for war among leading citizens. Many conducted public business for private motives. A faction of the Assembly ended up carrying out a coup against the rest. A few joined the city's enemies. Elsewhere, the loss of international peace so inflamed domestic factions that they literally consumed one another while overturning every aspect of human decency. Thucydides's paradigm for how "the whole Hellenic world was convulsed" was the revolution in Corcyra:

[W]ords had to change their ordinary meaning and to take that which now was given them. Reckless audacity came to be considered the courage of a loyal supporter; prudent hesitation, specious cowardice; moderation was held to be a cloak for unmanliness; ability to see all sides of a question incapacity to act on any. Frantic violence became the attribute of manliness; cautious plotting a justifiable means of self defense . . . until even blood became a weaker tie than party, from the superior readiness of those united by the latter to dare everything without reserve . . . revenge was held of more account than self preservation. . . . Oaths . . . only held good so long as no other weapon was at hand . . . success by treachery won the prize for superior intelligence. . . . The cause of all these evils was . . . lust for power arising from greed and ambition.[2]

balance — human qualities
tension
restraint
moderation

Greed, cruelty, and ambition had existed always. But, Thucydides tells us, wartime conditions had elevated first honor and then fear above calculations of self-interest.

Interest, which is least inimical of peace, should have brought the Peloponnesian War to a screeching halt any number of times. Thus, when some three hundred *Spartiates* became prisoners of the Athenians, Sparta conceded defeat readily. But in Athens, Alcibiades's sense of personal honor could not abide a peace for which he could not take credit. Similarly, after Athens's loss of its expeditionary force in Sicily, it was willing to accept almost any terms Sparta might have offered. But Sparta, flushed with victory and wanting permanently to rid itself of the fear of Athenian empire, decided to occupy Attica and to call on the Persian navy to help destroy Athens's seapower.

The Greeks had a heavy interest in the relative peace they lived, but, with few exceptions, they thought less of it than of fears, ambitions, and partisan interests. *They knew not or had forgotten any reason to do otherwise.* When the war's own logic took over, the peculiar balance of human qualities that had made free Greek *poleis* possible passed away.

The Fall of Europe

No less poignant was the process by which the nascent twentieth century's reigning ideas suppressed rational thoughts of interest, fed fears, perverted notions of honor, and started the war that undermined Europe's civilization. That war's consequences continue to kill.

The Europe of 1900 had lived mostly in peace since the wars of the French Revolution. Railroads, steam-driven industry, electricity, scientific agriculture, sanitation and medical science had made life healthier, more plentiful and comfortable for the masses than had been imagined possible. Education had spread. Especially in retrospect, we marvel at the polite manners, at the ease and freedom with which turn-of-the-century Europeans treated one another and mingled across national and class lines. The literature of the epoch confirms anecdotes from that time that show Europeans largely respecting unwritten codes of orderly behavior. In 1912 no one needed to enforce the rule "women and children first" on the Titanic's doomed passengers any more than anyone needed to enforce rules against indecent exposure. Obedience to laws, even military conscription, hardly needed to be enforced. The visitors to the Paris Exposition of 1900 did not need passports or identity papers. Nor did millions of Europeans, mostly poor, ask or obtain anyone's permission to emigrate to various parts of the New World, where they found even more opportunity for better lives. The monarchs who assembled for the funerals of Britain's Queen Victoria in 1901 and of Edward VII in 1910 behaved as members of the same family, which they were to a considerable extent. Surely, people had never had it so good, and had every reason to expect that life would continue getting better.

Few imagined that existing institutions, ideas, and habits would soon combine to produce the Great War, which swept away so much of a civilization so dependent on peace.

After Napoleon's 1815 defeat at Waterloo, Europeans had created nation-states in the image and likeness of Napoleon. The new states became the foci of popular affection, even worship. All organized themselves as Napoleon had France, and as Hegel had prescribed, with every house numbered so that bureaucratic government could pass its science to and collect sustenance from each. The states became the purveyors of education and sources of authority. They fostered the myth that people within their borders formed distinct races with different geniuses and destinies. All partook of Charles Darwin's ideology that life is an evolutionary struggle in which the fittest survive. Germany's General Friedrich von Bernhardi's statement that "the natural law . . . of the struggle for existence [mandates the choice between] world power or downfall" (vulgarized as "you must be either the hammer or the anvil") was only a more explicit avowal of the vitalism articulated by the leading philosophers of the age: Friedrich Nietzche and Henri Bergson.

Hence the European states imitated the Prussian General Staff: They lived in peace, but with minds primed for war.

The War of 1914–1918 was so fatal to European civilization precisely because it drew on that civilization's identification of morals and religion, of the good things in life, with the nation-state—and

because the nation-states had come to see themselves as moral abso-
lutes antagonistic to one another. The diplomatic histories of the
generation prior to the Great War show that the European states'
leaders were so single-minded in their pursuit of marginal advantages vis-à-vis one another that they ended up confusing marginal
interests with vital interests. Of them Thucydides might say that
their sense of honor and their fears obscured their interests.

Consider how briskly Socialist leaders in each country urged
their followers to join their countries' armies, though they had
vowed to keep the masses from becoming cannon fodder; how joy-
fully Frenchmen, Russians, Germans, British, Italians, and so forth
marched off to the slaughter, how unquestioningly their ecclesiastical authorities blessed their sacrifices; how little, *at first,* deadly discipline had to be applied to send men "over the top" to near-certain
death or maiming; how much pressure these men felt from their
families to give up their lives to duty. In short, European civilization called in its obligations to fight the Great War—and thus inval-
idated them.

During and immediately after the war, hate for the enemy briefly
obscured the obvious question: Why? But the 15 million dead, the
20 million crippled, the countless ex-soldiers who never forgot being
terrified, threatened, humiliated, mistreated, the countless women
condemned to husbandless and childless misery, the parents who had
lost children, the civilians who never forgot years of hunger, never
ceased imposing the question—all the more desperately because the
Great War was not followed by peace. France's Marshal Ferdinand
Foch's judgment "this is not peace, but an armistice for twenty years"
was as widely shared as it was accurate. Foch (1851-1929)

There was no peace because none of the warring parties ever had
a good idea of what peace they preferred and could sustain. And
then hate addled their judgment further. None discussed what the
practical consequences of specific readjustment of frontiers, what
any particular objective, was worth in terms of sacrifices of blood
and treasure. They stuck to generalities. Much less, once the conflict stalemated, did they imagine satisfactory compromises, in part
because compromising in terms of generalities is well nigh impossible. Finally, when the Untied States' intervention tipped the military

scales, President Woodrow Wilson's insistence on his abstract, self-contradictory schemes for perpetual peace removed any possibility of the real thing.

Were the losers to be guarded against by a system of alliances, or were they equally part of the international community? Both. Did the international community forswear war, or was it ready to wage it to maintain the last war's results? Both. Were all peoples to decide for themselves by whom they would be governed, or did the winners have the right to decide sovereigns and borders? Both. A generation of statesmen had invested themselves as well as their civilization in a massively destructive enterprise that they never thought through. Their mangled answers to the question "Why?" added to the war's bloody indictment of European civilization.

That civilization became a thing of the past as passions, resentments, and utopian longings overwhelmed its weakened remnants. After tearing at each other's vitals once again even more cruelly, Europeans were intellectually and morally spent—at peace with impotence.

But there could be no peace because the powerful passions and moral debilities that the twentieth century's wars engendered had infected the New World's Europeans as well as the Asians and Africans to whom Europeans had begun to spread their civilization.

Not since the Dark Ages has the world known warfare to which no one seemed to be seeking an end.

≪ 3 ≫

Defensor Pacis

Why is peace—and such civilization as may be built on it—so desirable as to be itself an argument against glories such as those of Rome and of Napoleon, against the wealth that may be gained by imposing extractive terms of trade upon subject peoples, against the violent pursuit of biological, cultural, or national destiny? In other words, what are the abstract reasons why, what are the principles on the basis of which, statesmen may be obliged to give primacy to concrete interests in peace over the pursuit of primacy? When is the game worth the candle and when not? By how much must the good results of a war overbalance the evils of its conduct to justify breaking the peace?

Augustus and Augustine

Once upon a time, these keys to Christian "just war" theory were staples of American statesmen's concerns. Not now. In 2013 the US government banned the teaching of "just war" theory in its academic venues because of its Christian origin.

Christian theology and political theory made the first intellectual effort to make peace the secular focus of civilization. Caesar Augustus's peace had been a brief interlude. From the days of Romulus (753 BC), Rome's internal order had rested on constant external war. Rome's civil wars broke out when powerful parties set aside the laws to prey on each other as they had preyed on foreigners. These wars' chief protagonists were the commanders of the long-service legions, which foreign conquests had made necessary, and on whom the soldiers depended for their welfare. Octavian's victory over all rivals not having established any basis for domestic peace, the imperial peace lasted only through the first two emperors. Thereafter, domestic and foreign strife fed on each other, gradually consuming the enormity that was Rome.

In the fifth century AD, Saint Augustine's *The City of God* had shown why Christians must be indifferent to the fate of the Roman Empire or of any earthly polity, and that the city of man is divinely ordained to provide the tranquility of order necessary for spiritual life. But, Jesus's admonition to the contrary, Constantine's adoption of Christianity as the empire's official religion had continued the ancient conflation between what man owes to Caesar and what he owes to God. Moreover, by the time Augustine wrote, the Dark Ages of tribal warfare were descending on Europe. Not until the thirteenth and fourteenth centuries did Thomas Aquinas, Dante Alighieri, and

> Marsilius of Padua develop a theory that tries to explain how peace may be organized.

The Christian faith sees no ultimate value in any collective secular enterprise, much less in war. Augustine left no doubt that, because earthly life is a pilgrimage toward communion with God, Christians are to have the least possible to do with any and all things that detract from that goal—even with things that are good in and of themselves, never mind with necessary evils. War is the worldliest of things, because it requires subordinating life itself to the primacy of some and the abasement of others. Also, war demands total concentration of human resources on a host of things that are evil in themselves, and does so despotically. Naturally, war crowds out of the human mind its proper focus on knowing, loving, and serving God. Hence Christian political thought has always emphasized maximizing peace and minimizing war. Augustine had explained the primacy of peace in terms of the natural law he had learned from Plato and Aristotle as well as from Christian theology.

But few paid much attention. The early Christians, as subjects of the Roman Empire (many of whom were in the legions) were mere instruments of un-Christian wars. Worse, after Christianity became the empire's official religion, the warring contenders were often nominally Christian. The problem did not go away when the barbarians invaded the Western empire beginning in the fifth century AD, because many of them were nominally Christian as well.

Franks, Longobards, and the Empire

Only gradually did some of the Germanic tribes recognize that their profession of Christianity required abandoning predatory behavior. They came to this recognition slowly by circuitous paths, including the correspondence between Theodolind, the Bavarian wife of two Longobard kings, and Pope Gregory I in the early seventh century. By the eighth century, the Longobard kings and the Frankish Carolingian dynasty had become familiar with Augustine's *The City of God*. Indeed, the Longobard king Liutprand (712–44) brought the scholar's bones to the church that would be his own tomb in Pavia, covered with a moving poem about "*vicini grata degebant pace per omnes*," "the peace that all [our] neighbors desired and [now] live," with thanks to Augustine "by whose doctrine the Church shines forth (*fulget*)."[1] Charlemagne himself, though illiterate, had *The City of God* read to him in Latin.

Yet there was no Christian statecraft properly speaking until the victory of Charlemagne's Franks over the Longobards in 774 AD. That victory, followed by feudal order rather than by slaughter, resulted in a Holy Roman Empire that fostered the Christian presumption for peace.

Charlemagne's empire did that because it neither tried to administer secular rule within, nor to impose spiritual authority over its parts. This, in a sense, ratified and sanctified the practice that had grown among the more Romanized Germanic tribes by the eighth century. The emperor claimed the right and duty to keep merely secular peace and justice among those parts. Thus under the Holy Roman Empire human beings for the first time—and the last until the founding of the United States—tried to institutionalize Jesus's command to distinguish duties to Caesar and duties to God.

The Church, its status now guaranteed, was supposed only to shepherd men spiritually. Nevertheless, under this system conflicts between nobles driven by merely secular interest, fear, and honor proved to be minor threats to peace compared to the papacy's unslakable thirst for temporal power. Separation between religion and politics, between power over things and the authority to pronounce on truth, good, and evil, is inherently rare and fragile.

Christian Statecraft

By the thirteenth century, when Thomas Aquinas wrote the medieval system's fullest explanation, its breakup was well advanced. Aquinas, like Augustine, understood secular government as divinely ordained to maintain the peace without which the highest objects of human desire cannot normally be pursued. He saw the Church as the body of Christ on earth, which alone can consecrate human life to its highest purposes in this world and to salvation in the next. Although Thomas understood both Church and empire to be autonomous in their own competencies, he judged that earthly rulers, like all men, are subject to the Church's judgments about faith and morals. The Church, wrote Thomas, must be careful lest its judgments on spiritual matters intrude upon legitimate earthly authority. But in the final analysis he thought that the pope is the earthly judge of his own reach, and that he has every right to declare earthly rulers illegitimate.

This of course is tremendous secular power. The papacy used it with malice aforethought. By the time Thomas died in 1274, the popes had used excommunication to start wars against the Hohenstaufen dynasty, wars that chased imperial power out of Italy and elected a pliant emperor from the house of Habsburg.

This, however, brought neither peace nor balance to the medieval system. Rather, it made the king of France the arbiter of papal elections, and made the papacy itself captive in Avignon, France. Soon, three popes were excommunicating and urging wars against one another. Reflecting on this, Dante Alighieri's *De Monarchia* (circa 1312) recalled that Church and empire were equally commissioned by God to reign over their respective spheres, but noted that the Church's corrupt overstepping of this law of nature was the biggest threat to peace. He concluded that because "it is plain that amid the calm and tranquility of peace the human race accomplishes most freely and easily its given work,"[2] that peace is earthly rulers' goal, both holy and natural.

In 1324 Marsilius of Padua's *Defensor Pacis* (Defender of Peace) gave the Christian conception of government its fullest definition. He drew the analogy between human society and the body of any animal, each part of which has its own necessary and coordinate function. The maintenance of peace and order belongs, by nature, to that part of human society that possesses the power physically to coerce. The part of society that possesses that power to enforce rules is also the part that makes those rules, the part that knows what temporal rules it needs. Hence, Marsilius wrote: "We declare that according to the truth and to the opinion of Aristotle, the lawgiver, that is, the primary essential and efficient source of law is the people, that is the whole body of citizens or a majority of them acting of their own free choice . . . under penalty of temporal punishment."[3] In short, Marsilius argues that there is a natural law that governs the health of the human body politic just as there is a natural law that governs the health of physical bodies. The body is distinct from the soul. The first of the body politic's laws is that it needs peace.

Thus anyone may judge any ruler's performance: Does he establish and defend peace, and thereby serve the people's interest? That judgment is practical and secular. Its authority is a more fundamental law of natural/divine origin, namely that the rulers exist for the sake of the ruled. That is, because secular rulers, like ecclesiastical authorities, are organs of the human commonwealth. They exist only to serve it. They may be interested in all sorts of things. But the people's primary secular interest is in peace and order. *This, then, is Christian theology's contribution to statecraft: serving the people's interest in peace and order is the standard, both earthly and divine, against which statesmen are to be judged.*

4

Patriot Kings

Christian statecraft was a brief interlude in mankind's perennial subjection. Aggrandizement, not peace, is the standard by which rulers ancient and modern tend to judge themselves. They tell the people, and some even believe, that their successes or failures are really the nation's, that subjects and even citizens are patriotic insofar as they contribute to the ruler's success or appearance thereof. Practically, patriotism means obedience to the ruler, regardless of peace or war, regardless of the quality of government. In Europe, the age of royal absolutism began in the mid-fourteenth century. In the succeeding four hundred years there were few attempts to explain why the interest of peoples in matters of war and peace is rightly superior to that of rulers, or why peoples ought to have a voice in such matters at all.

By 1324 when the *Defensor* was written, the Holy Roman Empire was becoming just another of Europe's secular powers, reduced to East-Central Europe. The greatest of these, the kings of France, England, and Spain, were about self-aggrandizement at home, the better to carry on war abroad. Kings claimed to be or simply acted as sovereigns of the Church. Prelates legitimized their claims to absolute authority by Divine Right over all aspects of life. Thus Catholic and Protestant churchmen became court chaplains—courtiers among others. This culminated in the wars of the sixteenth and seventeenth centuries that killed about a third of Germany's population. But though the level of violence declined after the Treaties of Westphalia of 1648, wars remained the main business of kings in the absence of ideas that valued peace, never mind of powers that might restrain war.

Divine Right vs. Peace

The principle of Divine Right ran contrary both to Christian theology and to the complex customary rules that feudal society had inherited from the Germanic tribes. Its simple jurisprudence, law is the king's will, trumped any notion of natural law and placed peoples at the service of kings. Throughout Europe the wars of the fourteenth through eighteenth century make sense, to the extent that they do, in terms of the perceived interest of kings in their own grandeur—what would be called *raison d'état*. The Middle Ages survived politically and intellectually to a significant extent only in England, where sovereigns never overrode the 1215 Magna Carta's medieval point that society would and should forcefully maintain its independence of royal rule and where, even under Henry VIII, the most authoritative published definition of the English body politic was Sir John Fortescue's (1394–1476) notion of a *dominium politicum et regale*. Hence no English king ever could claim that war and peace were his and his counselors' business alone because none could say, as did France's Louis XIV, "the state is me."

First in England in the late the seventeenth century, in the Bill of Particulars that led to Charles Stuart's beheading and in the Glorious Revolution, then in the eighteenth, the idea arose once more that the king must rightfully promote his people's interest, and that that interest lies in peace.

Viscount Bolingbroke preceded his writing of *The Idea of a Patriot King* (1738) by publishing a long, involved account of Europe's wars and intrigues, intended to strike the reader as a recitation of kings' business. But he dealt principally with the (then-recent) War of the Spanish Succession (1701–14) that had so deeply engaged British public opinion, and did so from the standpoint of the British people's interest. This led him to conclude that though it was worthwhile fighting to keep the Low Countries out of Louis XIV's hands, the Duke of Marlborough's victories at Blenheim (1704) and Ramillies

(1706) had secured this interest and that, thereafter, the people's interest lay in peace, not in another eight years of war. The ground thus prepared, Bolingbroke penned his *Idea,* an argument that a *properly patriotic* king pursues his people's interest first and foremost, and that pursuit of peace is a principal element of patriotism.

Bolingbroke

The *Idea* begins with a long attack on Machiavelli's notion of government, which had lent secular support to royal claims of absolute power. Then Bolingbroke contrasts *raison d'état* with patriotism. He made this radical departure from current wisdom as part of a general advocacy for the interests and mores of that vast majority of Englishmen who were neither part of the royal court nor its favorites—that is, on behalf of the country class as opposed to the court class. His point was all the more powerful because he was a Tory and the country was ruled by Whigs at the time.

> Great Britain is an island: and, whilst nations on the continent are at immense charge in maintaining their barriers, and perpetually on their guard, and frequently embroiled, to extend or strengthen them, Great Britain may, if her governors please, accumulate wealth in maintaining hers; make herself secure from invasions, and be ready to invade others when her own immediate interest, or the general interest of Europe require it. . . . When a great war begins, we ought to look on the powers of the continent, to whom we incline, like the two first lines, the *principes* and *hastati* of a Roman army: and on ourselves, like the *triarii,* that are . . . to be ready for the conflict whenever the fortune of the day, be it sooner or later, calls us to it, and the sum of things, or the general interest, makes it necessary.
>
> This is that post of advantage and honour. . . . If we neglect it, and dissipate our strength on occasions that touch us remotely or indirectly, we are governed by men who do not know the true interest of this island, or who have some other interest more at heart. . . .[1]

The argument for a presumption of restraint gained traction because, the Glorious Revolution of 1688 having established parliamentary sovereignty, foreign relations had become fully the Commons' business as well. Moreover, the revolution having set a Hanoverian dynasty on Britain's throne, the question of whether British foreign policy was properly focused on British rather than continental interests had become lively. Hence British public opinion (especially the Whig side) became intensely biased toward minimizing military and even political commitments on the European continent. The Whigs valued Parliament's enhanced role in foreign policy especially because they tended to equate the Crown's interest generally with war and that of the people generally with peace. *As we will see, British Americans inherited both the British Whigs' insular bias and their view that representatives of the people are likelier than kings to preserve peace.*

Turgot

Across the Channel, some of France's leading men were coming to similar conclusions from vastly different, but equally secular premises. Louis XVI's finance minister Anne-Robert-Jacques Turgot (1727–81) was among the greatest of his country's technocrats and eighteenth-century *Philosophes*. An economist and one of the original contributors to the *Encyclopedia*, Turgot was a systematic thinker. Raised in a merchant family, he early adopted the views of the Physiocrats, liberal economic thinkers who believed that man is moved by rational economic motives. As a royal administrator, his job was to improve the things he administered. A practitioner of efficiency, he became a leading theorist thereof, and one of history's most persuasive advocates of avoiding war, the most unproductive, the most wasteful and destructive, the most economically irrational, of human activities.

Like other Physiocrats, Turgot argued that, since the division of labor is as fundamental to economics internationally as it is on every other level, peace really is the natural interest, if not the natural state of mankind—the state that best befits its natural, rational inclinations and the condition most conducive to its progress. From this it follows logically that government's natural role is to secure peace. The prominence of such libertarian ideas in the cabinet of the grandson of Louis XIV, the cabinet so recently headed by those synonyms of *raison d'état,* Cardinals Richelieu and Mazarin, shows that natural law thinking about peace and war had survived its eclipse under royal absolutism.

Non-Physiocratic *Philosophes* such as the Abbé de Mably and Nicolas de Condorcet were outright pacifists largely out of disdain for monarchy. They simply assumed that all peoples want peace and that only crowned criminals do not. Hence Mably's learned commentaries on diplomacy advocated submitting treaties to popular ratification, while Condorcet's less temperate writings simply equated republics with peace.

Persons familiar with Greek and Roman history—for example, America's founders—needed no reminder that Divine Right of kings is only one of many rationales for subordinating the people's natural interest in peace to the *raison d'état* of self-aggrandizing governments. The Americans were also painfully aware that England's Glorious Revolution of 1688 had merely translated royal into parliamentary absolutism, while France's revolution of 1789 produced Robespierre's wars, to be finished by Napoleon. *Raison d'état* was almost as firmly entrenched in nineteenth- and twentieth-century Europe's self-worshiping states as in the Baroque age.

But ideas, like people, can migrate to more congenial circumstances. Thus it was that the idea that peace is human government's proper priority became a mainstay of the American founding generation's mentality in its Christian emphasis, as well as its economic-Physiocratic *and* its English-patriotic form. The Americans also followed the lead of liberals on both sides of the Channel (e.g., Montesqieu, who revered the British Constitution) by dividing the power over peace and war between executive and legislative functions. But as we shall see, their later successors' growing historical ignorance and self-indulgence eventually eclipsed those judgments.

5

A Right to Peace

The people's inalienable sovereignty over themselves was the American Revolution's intellectual point of departure—as was their sense of growing social and political alienation from their rulers. Before the 1763 end of the French and Indian Wars, Americans' resentment of British officials' highhandedness had been tempered by their need for military protection against French-supported Indian ravages. Thereafter, they came to see Britain's military presence, indeed the colonies' involvement in British imperial affairs, as the force behind Britain's economic and civil presumptions. This reinforced Americans' tendency to equate armies with oppression, and civil and economic rights with peace. President Dwight Eisenhower's 1961 farewell address was the last expression of this sentiment by a mainstream politician. But at the time of the founding, this reasoning *was* America's mainstream.

Nature and Nature's God

To explain why Americans were right to disobey Britain and disassociate from it, Thomas Jefferson and other revolutionaries argued that the king and Parliament of Great Britain had forfeited their authority by exceeding their powers to the point of making war on the people. The assertion of absolute sovereignty is tantamount to war. "Kings," wrote Jefferson in *A Summary View of the Rights of British America* (1774), "are the servants, not the proprietors of the people." Their service consists of being "the chief officer of the people, appointed by the laws, and circumscribed with definite powers."[1] The Americans argued that the king and Parliament had wantonly presumed to act as plenipotentiary proprietors rather than as guardians of man's natural right to enjoy the fruits of his labors in peace.

So much had this point of view already become conventional wisdom in America that British authorities' reminders of their power to unleash military force upon the Americans (e.g., by shutting the port of Boston) only further convinced the Americans that, in the words of a contemporary sermon, "[the king's] attempt to destroy the rights of the people destroys his right as king to reign over them, for according to his coronation oath he has no longer a right to the British throne, than he maintain inviolable firm the laws and rights of the people."[2] Foremost among these rights, said Pastor John Allen, is the undisturbed enjoyment of their own labors' fruits. In the same vein Jefferson wrote that "America was conquered, and her settlements made and firmly established at the expense of individuals. . . . For themselves they fought, for themselves they conquered, and for themselves alone they have right to hold."[3] In this, according to Jefferson, the Americans were no different from the Saxons who first came to the British Isles. The Norman Conquest of 1066 had enslaved them by war, but not by right.

Two years later, the Declaration of Independence asserted that Americans were entitled to break their bonds with Britain's king and Parliament because these had committed "a long train of abuses and usurpations" of the same kind as the ones that the Normans had imposed on the Anglo-Saxons. Many of these involved restrictions, enforced by war, on activities necessary for anyone's enjoyment of ordinary life: "quartering large bodies of troops among us . . . waging war against us . . . transporting large armies of foreign mercenaries . . . plundered our seas, ravaged our coasts, burnt our towns and destroyed the lives of our people . . . endeavored to bring on the inhabitants of our frontiers the merciless Indian savages . . . ." Hence, by "the laws of nature and nature's God," the Americans would henceforth "assume among the powers of the earth [a] separate and equal station." The American revolutionaries asserted that they, like every other people, had a natural right to live in peace according to their best judgment and capacities.

There is no evidence that it ever crossed the signers' minds that Americans might ever force their will upon other peoples as the British were doing to them. They asserted the right to make war in 1776 only for the purpose of living in peace.

Thomas Paine's *Common Sense* (1776) moved countless Americans to demand independence, including George Washington. Kings, Paine wrote, neither know nor care what is good for their people. The Bible, he reminded Americans, warns that kings' interest in their own greatness leads them to look at people as instruments for their personal passions and wars. God, through his prophets, told the Israelites that He alone is king, that *all* men are equally under Him, and hence that all should govern themselves by mutual agreement. *Common Sense* therefore argued Christian doctrine to its Christian audience: while the powers of the earth value primacy over others, God-fearing Americans should have other priorities, namely living in peace among themselves and with all nations.

It bolstered this with a Physiocratic point: Because peace is in everyone's interest, individuals and nations who live by consulting their interest will naturally get along with one another. Americans, Paine wrote, have no interest in anybody's quarrels, and should resist the temptation to join in Britain's quest for power. Paine concluded: "What have we to do with setting the world at defiance?" "Our plan is commerce." Many Americans believed along with Paine that peace is the natural state of republics, and that even monarchies would be willing to deal with America strictly on the pacific terms that Americans preferred. Of this, reality soon disabused them.

neutral independence

Just and Unjust Causes

The authors of the *Federalist Papers* were not such believers. They argued that America, like other nations, would have to earn peace through careful management of international affairs. Indeed, among the principal reasons for the Convention that produced the Constitution for the ratification of which the *Federalist Papers* were arguing was that foreign nations were not leaving America to live in peace. The merely confederated American states could not weigh in the balance of international affairs. The American people would have to earn their peace.

In *Federalist* #3, John Jay reminds Americans of how important it is to fulfill international obligations, and to settle disputes coolly and amicably, thus refraining from giving foreigners any "just causes" for war. Nevertheless, Jay makes clear in *Federalist* #4 that amicable behavior and self-restraint do not by themselves secure peace with foreign republics any more than with haughty monarchs. Any and all foreign powers may make up excuses, "unjust causes," for depriving Americans of peace. Commercial rivalries and countless other motives may lead even foreign republics to make intolerable demands upon America, unless the Americans are powerful enough to discourage them. United, the states of America would give less offense, and provide for themselves a more daunting defense.

More than a century later, Theodore Roosevelt would synthesize this formula for peace: "speak softly and carry a big stick." In short, America's founding generation believed they had a good, perhaps even unique, grasp of what nature grants to and demands from mankind. But they did not doubt that these rights and demands pertained to all mankind equally, and that their understanding neither added to nor subtracted from America's obligation to nature's laws.

6

America, Not Rome

exceptionalism

God Himself, it seemed, had destined the United States of America to be perhaps the greatest nation ever. Through sermons, the mass media of the day, America's spiritual and intellectual authorities explained to the people of what their greatness would consist. From the time of the very first settlements, Americans had regarded themselves as the new Israel, commissioned by God to show exemplary virtue, righteous obedience, and to reap unique rewards in the Promised Land. The North American continent was practically infinite, its obvious wealth untapped. Population was increasing faster than anyone thought possible. What should Americans do with all that bounty?   *expansion*

Happy Switzerland

On the occasion of the adoption of Massachusetts's constitution (drafted by John Adams, 1780) Boston divine Samuel Cooper preached that "righteousness exalteth a nation," that the Israelites had chosen to serve the Lord freely and "democratically," that Americans should do likewise, that righteous obedience to the Lord yields freedom, and that America's righteous freedom would guarantee its "rise to eminence." America's eminence would rival that of ancient Rome. But, said Cooper, "conquest is not indeed the aim of these rising states." Rather, its aim is to make North America, "a large portion of the globe," into a "seat of Christian virtue" to which we should "invite the injured and oppressed, the good and the worthy" of all nations so that they might share "a quiet and peaceable life in all godliness and honesty."

How should this be accomplished? By imitating "happy Switzerland," whose "independence is supported by force."[1] America's purpose was not to *do* anything exceptional, but to *be* something exceptional.

That something was to be peaceful to the maximum extent possible. To celebrate the 1783 end of the Revolutionary War, Yale's president, the Reverend Ezra Stiles, preached a sermon titled "The United States Elevated to Glory and Honor." The glory was to be the removal of impediments to human perfection through the "sweet and attractive chorus" of civil and religious liberty. Through this, "the Lord shall have made his American Israel high above all nations that he shall have made." Navigation will "carry the American flag around the globe, and display the thirteen stripes at Bengal and Canton, on the Indus and the Ganges." The prophecy of Daniel shall be fulfilled: "a universal traveling to and fro, and knowledge shall be increased [so as to] illumine the world with truth and liberty."[2] In a similar vein, Elhanan Winchester preached in 1792 that the United States of America "have the happiness of teaching the world" the most important lessons of human life, namely how, by living in peace, a whole continent can be turned into a monument to the glory of God: "Behold the whole continent . . . behold the glory of God."[3]

Clearly, the notion of isolating America from foreign nations was as foreign to the founding generation as was that of conquering them. The Americans were immigrants or recent descendants of folks who had left other countries hoping for a better life here. They wanted to make their bet pay off, to prove that leaving the old country had been a good choice. America was their final destination, where they looked forward to being joined by others like themselves. That was the greatness to which they aspired. They had come to America to leave their home countries' quarrels behind, and were fully occupied in reaping the rich harvests of peace.

How rich? It is difficult for today's Americans to comprehend how unique America's abundance of food was *and is*, how foreign to the human experience it is for all to eat their fill. So much better fed were

Americans than Europeans that, already during the Revolutionary War, American soldiers were an average of two inches taller than their opponents. Hence it would have been surprising had Americans wanted to deviate from the choice for peace and commerce that had *?* brought them so much prosperity.

In sum, religion, interest, and prudence combined on the level of ideas to confirm the primacy of peace upon the American mind. Securing peace through policy was another matter.

Squaring the Circle

Even Thomas Paine, the author of *Common Sense*'s formula for American foreign policy, "our plan is commerce," was acutely aware that Americans would have to use force and contract alliances with kings in order to secure their grand, peaceful future. The second part of *Common Sense* argues for the construction of an American navy, and gives a detailed account of how that should be done. The Continental Congress placed Paine at the head of its committee on foreign relations, which confided to John Adams the responsibility for framing the American people's proposal to France for waging war jointly against Britain.

The Congress debated the details of *how to square their unani-* [*model treaty*] *mous preference for limiting foreign relations to peaceful commerce with their unanimous realization that this would not be enough.* In sum, the colonists' decision to make war was of one piece with the decision to declare independence—decisions of the greatest caliber imaginable. All recognized that *reconciling bedrock principles with bedrock necessity belongs by nature to the people's elected representatives.*

The Constitution's framers did not have to be convinced that the executive is likelier to choose war than peace, because war enhances its powers and that it often serves narrow interests close to it. That is why the Constitutional Convention of 1787 placed the responsibility for war—namely for departing from the American people's sovereign interest in peace—squarely and exclusively in the Congress of the United States. Securing peace through war would always be divisive and never straightforward.

In the *Federalist*, James Madison (#41) and Alexander Hamilton (#25) explained that decisions about war and peace are *legislative* by nature because the people can come together about their common interest only through their representatives' dialogue. It would always be hard for many to set aside their particular ambitions. In 1838, the young Abraham Lincoln pointed to the danger posed by the presence among peaceful Americans of persons like Julius Caesar and Napoleon, who belong to "the family of the lion, the tribe of the eagle," whose ambitions peace cannot satisfy. To avoid Rome's glorious misery, America would have to try hard and be lucky. It did and it was, for a while.

the fascist impulse
the bellicose few

≪ 7 ≫

Washington's Peace

The Revolutionary War of 1775–83 was almost as much a war between Americans as a war between Americans and British. In 1794 a tax rebellion in Pennsylvania was so serious as to require the president of the United States to ride at the head of an army to suppress it. That the United States emerged from these trials united in peace is due in no small part to George Washington's single-minded focus on achieving precisely that result. He understood of what that peace would consist. That understanding informed his conduct of military affairs. Let us look closer.

Like Lincoln some four score years later, Washington in 1775 faced statesmanship's most daunting problem: how to reconcile a nation's parts by defeating one of them. It helped Washington (like Lincoln) that he had not started the fight. Britain had repeatedly rebuffed the colonies' pleas for redress of grievances. Britain had imposed martial law on Boston and had attempted to disarm its environs. Some Americans were helping those authorities against fellow Americans, while others had prevailed on Washington to lead resistance to the British. From the outset, General Washington refrained from any sort of offensive against American Tories, discouraged violence against them, and expressed readiness to accept at face value anyone's declaration of allegiance to the patriot cause.

Victory and Peace

As in all wars, many people's allegiances depended on which side's forces were in control of their area. Washington presumed all Americans to be patriots unless they went out of their way to prove themselves otherwise. Thus, after his troops had conquered New Jersey, where many had sworn allegiance to the British crown, Washington issued a proclamation that, after brandishing supreme authority, asked all such people simply to go home and be good Americans. The sense of this was that since victory would consist of peace, punishment would amount to the continuation of war. Washington wanted to end it. Still, forty thousand Tories had so burned their bridges with their neighbors that they chose to leave the United States. But that was their doing, their choice. Washington behaved similarly in the face of Pennsylvania's Whiskey Rebellion of 1794. Alexander Hamilton tried to persuade Washington to teach the rebels a harsh lesson. But while Washington saw the need to ride into the area at the head of a large army, he did so brandishing plenary pardons. He hanged no one. The absolute priority of peace at home was the lesson he wanted to teach.

That proved harder to do in politics than in military matters, because the people do not always know their own interest. Beginning in 1792, France's Revolution and its subsequent war against the rest of Europe so set Americans against one another as almost to turn domestic factions into warring nations. Washington knew that neutrality in foreigners' quarrels, necessary as it was to America' s international peace, was even more essential domestically because the American people's physical mobility, ethnic and religious diversity, provide unusually weak immunological resistance to the spread of strife. Americans already had more than enough reasons to divide into factions and to increase mutual animus.

A decade earlier, in his circular letter to the states preceding his resignation as commander of the army, Washington had urged his fellow countrymen to look upon the rest of the world from an American perspective, and upon themselves as Americans. Washington often said: "we have a national character to establish." By this he meant both that Americans should adopt righteous habits, and that they should think and act as a national whole.

War Spurs Faction

The French Revolution and its wars showed how correct Washington's fears had been and how difficult it would be to build "national character," indeed to maintain domestic peace—never mind international neutrality—in the face of the American people's affections and distastes for the foreign warring parties. The leaders of the contending domestic factions were none other than the principal members of Washington's own cabinet, who happened to loathe each other personally: Secretary of State Thomas Jefferson thought well of the French Revolution, suggested that America's own domestic life should be inspired to some extent by its ideals, and tried to shape US foreign policy in France's favor. He thought Secretary of the Treasury Alexander Hamilton a royalist. Hamilton for his part saw the French Revolution as an abomination, thought Jefferson a Jacobin, admired the British constitution, and wanted at least to make sure that America did not hurt Britain's cause.

By the 1793 proclamation of neutrality, Washington intended to compose the two factions' differences. But there is no democratic remedy for a blindly impassioned *demos*. Hence the proclamation became the occasion for the two parties to divide the country ever more passionately between fully stated positions.

A sector of public opinion felt that the United States should weigh in somehow on France's side out of gratitude for the essential role France had played in America's fight for independence and because of the 1778 Franco-American treaty of amity and commerce. Alexander Hamilton's *Pacificus* and *Americanus* essays argued that the treaty bound America only to support France in the West Indies, which would be of marginal importance to France but would involve America in a war with Britain that might well end up in our loss of independence. Thus, the treaty did not oblige America to give up peace and hazard its own existence. Jefferson called this argument clever, but really a screen for a pro-British bias.

The truth of the matter was that, in the mid-1790s, siding with France meant war with Britain, whose forbearance at sea was essential to America's peaceful commerce. To secure that forbearance,

President Washington's envoy, John Jay, negotiated a treaty of commerce with Britain. Jefferson resigned from the cabinet. The tenor of his party's opposition may be seen in its slogan: "Damn John Jay! Damn everyone who won't damn John Jay!! Damn anyone that won't put lights in his windows and sit up all night damning John Jay!!!"

Meanwhile, France's retaliation against the United States for the Jay Treaty led to a quasi-war at sea, the containment of which President John Adams barely managed. Adams's diplomacy was successful because it was backed by warships: "*si vis pacem, para bellum*"—if you want peace, prepare for war.

Washington never had to be reminded of that maxim. Hard experience had also taught him that since the passions of conflict tend to get out of control once loosed, peace is preserved most efficiently by avoiding the near occasions of conflict. So, in a manner that is not to be forgotten, Washington's Farewell Address explained the importance of what Theodore Roosevelt later called "speaking softly." We must keep in mind that Washington intended to instruct the American people at large even more than the officials who would succeed him. The people's passions were pushing America to the brink of joining a world at war and of going to war among themselves. He meant to teach the people how to bridle those passions.

The Great Rule of Peace

Washington's opening point, "Observe good faith and justice towards all nations; cultivate peace and harmony with all," contains the essence of the matter: The United States' concern for its own peace, its own interest, is so paramount as to make America indifferent to the nature of any and all other nations. For Washington, monarchies, despotisms, ancient civilizations, savage tribes, were all alike in one essential respect: They were not American. Their business was theirs, not ours. *Our overriding business with regard to them was to have no trouble with them.* Washington counseled that insofar as our paths crossed with theirs, peace and harmony were to be our objective, to be pursued with good faith and justice. It is important to note that *Washington named no substantive objectives for American foreign relations—none. Only peace.* And to achieve this, any nation of any character might be of use to America, as Russia proved useful during the Revolution and later during the Civil War.

Washington explained that "peace and harmony" with foreigners promotes something even more important, namely peace among Americans:

> In the execution of such a plan nothing is more essential than that permanent inveterate antipathies against particular Nations and passionate attachments for others should be excluded; and that in place of them just & amicable feelings towards all should be cultivated. . . . The Nation, prompted by ill will & resentment sometimes impels to War the Government, contrary to the best calculations of policy. . . . So likewise, a passionate attachment of one Nation for another produces a variety of evils. Sympathy for the favourite nation, facilitating the illusion of an imaginary common interest, in cases where no real common interest exists, and infusing into one the enmities of the other, betrays the former into a participation in the quarrels & Wars of the latter, . . . And it gives to ambitious, corrupted, or deluded citizens (who devote themselves to the favourite Nation) facility to betray, or sacrifice the interests of their own country, . . . [S]uch attachments are particularly alarming to the truly enlightened and independent Patriot. How many opportunities do they afford to tamper with domestic factions, to practice the arts of seduction, to mislead public opinion, to influence or awe the public Councils!

From this, Washington drew his "great rule":

> The Great rule of conduct for us, in regard to foreign Nations is in extending our commercial relations to have with them as little political connection as possible . . . even our Commercial policy should hold an equal and impartial hand: neither seeking nor granting exclusive favours or preferences; consulting the natural course of things; diffusing & deversifying by gentle means the streams of Commerce, but forcing nothing. . . .

The meaning of "as little *political* connection as possible" may be seen in the words "forcing nothing." In other words, Americans should relate to other nations insofar as they agreed freely and easily, insofar as possible avoiding situations in which either side forced or felt forced. This of course is very much in accord with the theory according to which human society is based on free contract.

Washington's advice to an America transfixed by the wars of the French Revolution was to think less of them than of America itself: "Europe has a set of primary interests, which to us have none, or a very remote relation. . . . Why forego the advantages of so peculiar a situation? Why quit our own to stand upon foreign ground? Why, by interweaving our destiny with that of any part of Europe, entangle our peace and prosperity in the toils of European Ambition, Rivalship, Interest, Humour or Caprice?"[1]

In other words, the more America could mind its own business, the better off it would be.

8

Impotence, Honor, and War

President Thomas Jefferson and his successor James Madison did their best to mind America's business. France's violence against American shipping had brought them to see the value in Washington's, Hamilton's, and Adams's preference for noninvolvement as the path to peace. Jefferson and Madison ended up damning both Britain and France, and spent a dozen years trying to disentangle the United States from their quarrel. They failed; and ended up losing the peace because the tools they used, various forms of trade embargoes, were insufficient to the task. Unlike Adams, they neglected to build up the navy and to prepare for war to gain at least some respect for America's peace. In the meanwhile, they inadvertently fostered domestic strife.

Almost always, staying out of other peoples' quarrels requires being ready, willing, and able to mount a quarrel of one's own. Neutrals want to be friends with both belligerents. But each belligerent naturally regards third parties strictly from the standpoint of its own interest. Third parties may have no "dog in the fight." But the fighting dogs demand that neutrals act as allies lest they be treated as enemies. Hence the neutrals end up hurt by both sides unless they can hurt one or both of those who would hurt them. That means either retaliating forcefully against each belligerent's hostile acts, or allying with whichever of the belligerents is the least harmful.

Jefferson and Madison eschewed the first because they did not value military power, and the second because they had become even more averse to alliances than Washington. In response to France's seizure of American cargoes and Britain's seizure of American seamen along with cargoes, Jefferson imposed a commercial embargo on both. In doing that, he reprised the mistake of the American colonists of 1774–75 who had trusted that a trade embargo would convince the British to reduce their pressure on Americans. Then Jefferson and Madison doubled down on their bet by cutting off imports from both states via the 1809 Nonintercourse Act and its companion bill.

But the pacific path did not lead to peace in 1808 any more than it had in 1775. The British did not recognize US citizenship, maintained forts on the Great Lakes in violation the peace of 1783, and subsidized Indian wars against the American frontier. In 1812 British-armed Indians massacred the settlement that would become Chicago.

Jefferson and Madison had to relearn the hard way what Washington had taught: failure to secure peace abroad would undermine peace at home. Jefferson's fruitless attempt at "peaceable coercion" heightened strife between Republicans and Federalists, eastern and western states. Republicans from the latter, least hurt by the diminution of trade, reacted most strongly to the slights to national honor while the Federalist northeast, dependent as it was on overseas commerce, nearly seceded from the Union at the Hartford Convention of 1814. Congress's declaration of war resulted from deliberation and vote, all right. But the deliberation was a dozen years too late, and the vote was partisan. Worse, the partisans of war in 1812 had not been partisans of, or even conversant with, military power. "War hawks" such as J. C. Calhoun and Henry Clay spoke loosely about redeeming "American honor," stopping Indian ravages, the impressments of American sailors, and conquering Canada. But how? With what?

Hence President Madison and the Republican Party plunged America into the War of 1812 almost by default: as the alternative to corrosive, dispiriting, national dishonor. They had no plan for achieving peace, only the hope of securing enough respect on which to found future peace. The United States' invasion of Canada was a failure, though not as embarrassing as the British Army's burning of Washington, DC. The overall military debacle notwithstanding, America's efforts, including successes in ship-to-ship combat and Andrew Jackson's overwhelming victory in the defense of New Orleans, were enough to show that the country had great strategic depth and defensive reserve. That proved to be just enough to earn the bare minimum of respect and cohesion indispensable to peace.

9

American Geopolitics

John Quincy Adams (1767–1848), secretary of state and sixth president of the United States, filled in the founding generation's framework for international affairs and established paradigms of statesmanship that endured to the end of the nineteenth century. They are worth recalling today. The world's nations, their different characters and concerns, would be kept peacefully at arm's length and would be interesting in proportion to their proximity to our borders. Americans would not interfere in other peoples' business and make very sure that they did not interfere in ours, thereby applying the golden rule to international affairs. Adams's chief interest was maintaining America's character as defined by the Declaration of Independence, thus enabling moral and material progress.

Adams spoke from experience. At age 10 he had accompanied his father on missions to France and Holland. When it looked as though a British frigate might intercept their ship, the boy shouldered a musket along with the marines. He served as his father's secretary and learned the local languages. His first formal diplomatic assignment, to Russia, came at age 14. By 1817, when he became James Monroe's secretary of state, he had been the US representative to the Netherlands, Britain, Russia, and Prussia, had negotiated the end to the War of 1812, and knew French, German, Spanish, Italian, Dutch, and Russian in addition to Latin and Greek. In 1793 he had defended George Washington's policy of neutrality and been appointed by him as minister to the Netherlands. He had parted ways with the Federalist Party because he supported Jefferson's Louisiana Purchase (1803) and Embargo Act (1807). In short, he personified knowledge of the world as well as patriotism and commitment to peace.

Priorities

A few examples show Adams's practical proclivities. On July 18, 1816, as British Foreign Secretary Lord Castlereagh was briefing him on Britain's latest negotiation with the Dey of Algiers, Adams remarked that had the United States a navy but one-third the size of Britain's, no one would hear of the Barbary pirates ever again. He believed that the pirates should be exterminated because safety on the seas is basic to civilization. By the same token, because Adams believed that slavery is a gross violation of natural law, in 1820 he persuaded the Monroe cabinet to impose hanging as the penalty for importing slaves. In 1824, setting aside a half-century's resentment of British seizures of US ships, he negotiated a treaty authorizing the British navy to search US flag vessels suspected of slave trading. Concern for America's character always informed his advocacy of American greatness. That is why though Adams had supported the Louisiana Purchase at the risk of his career; though he had been responsible for the acquisition of the Floridas and had negotiated the 1819 treaty that extended US borders to the Pacific, he opposed Texas's several applications to join the United States because its acceptance of slavery would degrade America's character and hazard its peace.

Adams set forth his image of the United States most succinctly in his July 4, 1821, speech, which depicts the Declaration of Independence as the culmination of the human spirit's climb out of kings' and popes' millennial oppression of bodies, minds, and souls. Englishmen had forced their kings to grant a few freedoms. But for the most part they believed that freedoms are gifts, not rights. The human spirit, however, continued to push against this ignorance. Technical advances in navigation and the arts opened new worlds, while the Lutheran Reformation uncovered anew man's direct relationship to God.

England's most enlightened citizens brought mankind's accumulated wisdom to the New World. Here they compacted with one another how they should live, and purchased land from the natives. "The slough of brute force was entirely cast off. All was with unbiased consent, all was the agreement of soul with soul." The ensuing Declaration of Independence is "a beacon on the summit of the mountain to which all the inhabitants of the earth may turn their eyes . . . a light of admonition to the rulers of men, a light of salvation and redemption to the oppressed. . . . This declaration holds out to the subject and to the sovereign the extent and the boundaries of their rights and duties." As a result of the Declaration, the American people became "civilized men and Christians, in a state of nature . . . bound by the laws of God . . . by the laws of the Gospel . . . habits of hardy industry . . . by the general sentiments of social equality, by pure and virtuous morals. . . ."

How do such a people compare with and relate to the rest of the world? Adams acknowledges Europe's superiority in music and sculpture, as well as in the arts of destruction, but reminds his audience that America's contribution is to the useful sciences, such as the steamboat and the cotton gin, to the practices that improve human life. Adams stresses America's contribution to peace: America

has in the lapse of nearly a half century, without a single exception, respected the independence of other nations while asserting and maintaining her own. She has abstained from interference in the concerns of others even when the conflict has been for principles to which she clings, as if to the last vital drop that visits the heart. . . . She well knows that by once enlisting under banners other than her own, were they even the banners of foreign independence, she would involve herself beyond the power of extrication, in all the wars of interest and intrigue, of avarice envy, and ambition, which assume the colors and usurp the standard of freedom. The fundamental maxims of her policy would insensibly change from liberty to force.

Adams concludes by likening America to the Athens of Themistocles, which, he implied, became great through wisdom. America's glory, unlike Rome's, is to be liberty, not dominion. "She has a spear and a shield: but the motto upon her shield is *Freedom, Independence, Peace*."[1]

"The Laws of Political Gravitation"

Adams pursued peace by diplomacy conformant to natural law. In 1818, President Monroe had sent General Andrew Jackson to protect American settlers against raiders, a mixture of Indians and escaped Negro slaves, who were killing Americans and trading their booty at a fort in Spanish West Florida established by two British adventurers. Jackson pursued the raiders, killing as many as he could, destroyed the fort, and ceremoniously hanged the British. Spain protested her sovereignty, upsetting President Monroe's cabinet. Adams brought the cabinet to agree to frame the matter thus: Spain, as Florida's sovereign, was responsible for what happened on its territory. But Spain had allowed war to be waged on Americans from its territory. Because Spain was not securing America's peace, Americans had to do it. Hence Jackson had done the right thing. If Spain wanted Jackson to withdraw, it should send to Florida a force that would police it, reassuring the United States that it would maintain peace.

In 1823, Europe was abuzz with rumors that the Holy Alliance of Russia, Prussia, Austria, and Bourbon France was about to mount an expedition to recover newly independent South America to Spanish sovereignty. Britain asked the United States to join in declaring opposition to such a venture. President Monroe, having consulted with former Presidents Jefferson and Madison, was inclined to agree, and proposed to include a stinging denunciation of the Holy Alliance in his annual address. At the same time Russia, which had enquired of the US about a possible expansion of its possessions on the Pacific coast of North America, affirmed the universal validity of the tsar's claim to rule by Divine Right. Adams convinced Monroe that America's position should reflect America's peculiar character and hence particular interest, while avoiding criticism of European matters, and that this would be a good occasion to address the United States' policy in the Western Hemisphere and vis-à-vis the rest of the world.

That policy, said Adams, should proceed from the United States' own character and interest. Britain's proposal for a joint declaration, which could not help but proceed from Britain's own interest in monarchy, had also asked the United States to pledge never to annex Cuba. The answer that Adams drafted for Monroe, which became known as the Monroe Doctrine, answered both Britain and Russia. It proceeded from the fact that preserving independent republicanism at home was chief among US interests. The United States noted that the peoples of the Americas had chosen republican forms of government, and that for any European power to transfer its form of government to any part of the Americas would be against the nature of things and against US interests as well. For its part, the United States had "not interfered and shall not interfere" with European affairs.

Thus, *recognition of fundamental differences, along with mutual forbearance, was the Monroe Doctrine's practical essence.*

Adams's reasoning is most succinct in his April 28, 1823, letter of instruction to America's minister to Spain, Hugh Nelson.

[T]he first and paramount duty of the government is to maintain peace amidst all the convulsions of foreign wars, and to enter the lists as parties to no cause, other than our own.

In the maritime wars of Europe, we have, indeed, a direct and important interest of our own; as they are waged upon an element which is the common property of all. . . . To all maritime wars Great Britain can scarcely fail of becoming a party. . . . Whatever may be the issue of [the impending war between France and Spain] it may be taken for granted that the dominion of Spain upon the American continents, North and South, is irrecoverably gone. But the islands of Cuba and Puerto Ricos still remain . . . dependent on her, that she possesses the power of transferring her own dominion over them, to others. These islands, from their local position, are natural appendages to the North American continent; and one of them, Cuba, [has, for many reasons] an importance in the sum of our national interests, with which no other foreign territory may be compared, and little inferior to that which binds the different members of this Union together.[2]

Adams then notes that were the apple that is Cuba to be severed from Spain, the tree from which it hangs, the "laws of political gravitation" dictate that it would "gravitate towards the North American Union." Nevertheless, "it is obvious" that "formidable objections to the extension of our territorial dominions beyond the sea present themselves to the first contemplation of the subject." Foremost of those objections is the upsetting effect on the body politic of ingesting something essentially foreign and indigestible, however alluring. Adams concludes that though annexing Cuba would be neither right nor practicable for the United States, the island's importance makes it imperative to avoid its being transferred to Great Britain.

Adams's peaceful paradigm of American geopolitics, then, consists of three rules: first, assert America's identity and interests in ways that respect others' identities and interests. Second, prevent troublesome forces from getting among us or even near us (even forgoing voluntary adhesions). And third, what is nearest is dearest.

10

What Greatness?

It follows, especially for large countries, that avoiding quarrels at home is most important to living peacefully. After the War of 1812 had shown the United States' unconquerable reservoir of defensive strength, America's peace was endangered not by any foreign nation, but by its own statesmen's inadequacies. Abraham Lincoln said it best in his Lyceum Address of 1838: "At what point shall we expect the approach of danger? . . . All the armies of Europe, Asia, and Africa combined with a Buonaparte at their head, disposing of all the world's treasure (our own excepted) in their military chest could not by force take a drink from the Ohio or make a track upon the Blue Ridge in a trial of a thousand years."[1] Lincoln then pointed to the increasingly violent partisan divisions that foreshadowed the Civil War that would kill some two percent of the population.

Moral and economic conflicts over slavery were dividing Americans into two nations, both of which were losing contact with the founders' priorities. Both South and North were thinking in ways that implied very different versions of the good life, and that made peace ever less likely between them. The war against Mexico of 1846–48, and the national controversy about what kind of greatness Americans should seek, were manifestations of this.

By the time John L. O'Sullivan published his poetic rendition of the J. Q. Adams view of America in *The United States Democratic Review,* 1839, his words glossed over the profound partisan differences that had grown up about America's character, American greatness, and America's reach—differences that led to war with Mexico in 1846 and between the states in 1861:

> . . . the nation of many nations is destined to manifest to mankind the excellence of divine principles; to establish on earth the noblest temple ever dedicated to the worship of the Most High—the Sacred and the True. Its floor shall be a hemisphere—its roof a firmament of the star studded heavens, and its congregation an Union of many Republics, comprising hundreds of happy millions.[2]

The notion that our Union could be hemispheric was plausible hyperbole. Adams and the founding generation had imagined that perhaps Cuba or some parts of Mexico and Canada might someday choose to join the United States. For the founders and Adams, however, any new peoples coming into the Union would have to have precisely the same rights and obligation as the original thirteen, as specified by the Northwest Ordinance of 1789. But O'Sullivan and the Democratic Party to which his magazine belonged, the party of Andrew Jackson and then James Polk and then Stephen Douglas, was deliberately silent about what the character of these "republics" would be, as well as about how they might come into the Union. This was true also of many in the Whig Party.

Greatness and Size

Stephen Douglas, the Democratic Party's leader in the 1850s, famously argued in his 1858 debates with Abraham Lincoln: "I tell you increase, and multiply, and expand, it is the law of this nation's existence. You cannot limit this great republic by mere boundary lines, saying 'thus far shalt thou go and no further.' Any one of you gentlemen might as well . . . in order to prevent [the growth of a son twelve years old] put a hoop around him to keep him to his present size. . . . Either the hoop must burst and be rent asunder, or the child must die. . . ." Later in the same year, Douglas explained further: "The more degrees of latitude and longitude embraced by our republic, the better . . . making us the greatest planting as well as the greatest manufacturing, the greatest commercial as well as the greatest agricultural power on the globe."[3] But Douglas and those whom he led were clear that the associated "republics" would not necessarily recognize equal civil and political rights in all their citizen members.

Lincoln, for his part, summed up the matter thus in the Galesburg debate:

> If Judge Douglas' policy upon this question succeeds . . . the next thing will be a grab for the territory of poor Mexico, and invasion of the rich lands of South America . . . I don't know whether the judge will be in favor of the Mexican people that we get with it settling [the slavery question] for themselves . . . because we know the judge has a great horror of mongrels, and I understand that the people of Mexico are most decidedly a race of mongrels. And I suppose . . . that when we get Mexico he will be in favor of these mongrels settling this question, which would bring him somewhat into collision with his horror of an inferior race.[4]

Although Negro slavery embittered the clash between different visions of American greatness, these did not flow necessarily from sentiments about Negro slavery. *Would the good life, would peace, flow from the exercise of power, or would it flow from agreement that human equality requires government by unconstrained consent of the governed?* That was the essence of the division. It remains so in our time. Indeed, some advocates of slavery held fast to the founders' and Adams's view that America's greatness had less to do with power than with virtue, while some who were indifferent to slavery, like Stephen Douglas, or even opposed to it, thought in terms of power.

Greatness and Virtue

Thus Alexander Stephens of Georgia, who became the Confederacy's vice president, and who famously explained that Negro slavery was its "cornerstone," had opposed the Mexican war along with his friend and colleague Abraham Lincoln of Illinois, and had given a heartfelt explanation why wanton war-making is ruinous to America. ". . . lust for power . . . aggression, violence, and licentiousness . . . would soon sweep over all law, all order and the Constitution itself." Were America to dominate other peoples, it would lose "that high order of moral and political integrity without which no republic can stand." True greatness, Stephens argued, means "the increase and diffusion of knowledge among men . . . the progress of intellect over matter, the triumph of mind over animal propensities; the advancement of feelings and good will among the nations of the earth; the cultivation of virtue and the pursuit of industry . . . every thing that elevates, ennobles, and dignifies man."[5] Neither Lincoln nor John Quincy Adams would have changed a word.

By contrast, some anti-slavery Americans, including New York's Walt Whitman, now advocated annexing all of Mexico forcefully to bring the blessings of good government to people who had known only misrule. Thus, said Whitman, Americans would "regenerate the world by asserting the privileges of humanity over the accidents of birth and fortune."[6] The Mexicans were "aborigines" who would do better guided by us than they would by themselves. In Philadelphia, Admiral Robert F. Stockton proposed guiding "these wretched people" with a kindly hand "into the fold of republicanism." These opponents of Negro slavery who scoffed at southern masters' claims of benevolence were keen to exercise power over other peoples without their consent because *they*, the truly benevolent, the truly enlightened, would do so to the benefit of their subjects. They bemoaned the violence necessary to hold slaves, but imagined that they could rule foreign "aborigines" in peace. This attitude continues in our time.

In the end, neither the Polk administration nor the Whig opposition endorsed the movement to take "All Mexico" largely because the notion of ruling others without their consent was so repugnant to most Americans. Most Americans also did not approve of merely seizing even Mexico's mostly unpopulated northern end. That is why the Polk administration covered its taking that big chunk of Mexico first by hapless schemes to purchase it, then by justifying hostilities with transparently false claims of Mexican aggression. Finally, after defeating Mexico, Polk paid to its government the price that it had offered for purchase. Hypocrisy is the price that vice pays to virtue.

Far from settling the issue of what peace the American people would enjoy, the Mexican War's outcome exacerbated it. Peace within the American South had always been hostage to preventing or crushing slave revolts—much as Sparta's peace had been—and Southerners had always believed that their peace required non-slave states to shield them by returning fugitive slaves. But the addition of new territory raised the prospect that enough new anti-slavery states might be added to amend the Constitution to abolish slavery. Hence Southerners pressed to allow slavery in federal territories as well as to take slave-holding Cuba.

Growing moral estrangement overshadowed issues of policy. In the North, as the "All Mexico" movement had shown, there had grown a sense of moral superiority and therefore of moral duty to confess others' sins and then forcibly to improve the sinners— starting with the slave-holding Southerners. These, for their part, increasingly regarded the Northerners as economic exploiters (the tariff) and would-be tyrants. That explains why the 94 percent of Southerners who owned no slaves ended up fighting the North as doggedly as did the slave masters.

In short, by the 1850s all too many Americans were more concerned with disputes among themselves than with peace. Lincoln's 1838 "Young Men's Lyceum Address" had urged Americans to value the law's peaceful resolution of disputes above the disputes' substance. Lincoln, while protesting the evil of slavery, affirmed his commitment to respect property in slaves by pointing out that a power extralegal enough to turn slaves into free men could also turn free men into slaves. Lincoln's vision of peace was in the minority. It usually is.

11

Lincoln's Peace

The Civil War's intellectual bookends, Lincoln's two inaugural addresses, explain how peace slipped from his hands and how he sought to seize it again. His address to Congress on July 4, 1861, explained how he would go about doing so.

The First Inaugural's bulk is a series of protestations about and pledges of disinterest in any and all acts that any reasonable Southerner might find offensive enough to oppose by force. Then Lincoln argues that the South would gain none of its objectives by forcibly separating, because the Union and the Confederacy, unlike a divorcing couple, could not move away from one another physically: "Suppose you go to war, you cannot fight always; and when, after much loss on both sides, and no gain in either, you cease fighting, the identical old questions, as to terms of intercourse, are again upon you."[1] It is easier, Lincoln argued, to make laws among friends than to make treaties between aliens. Lincoln's last words are such as any lover might say to a beloved whose departure he wishes to delay: "I am loath to close. We are not enemies, but friends. We must not be enemies. Though passion may have strained, it must not break our bonds of affection." Lincoln then looks forward to the time when "the mystic chords of memory" will be touched once again "by the better angels of our nature."

Lincoln asked the Southern states to do nothing offensive, in exchange for his doing nothing offensive. No federal official would discriminate against Southerners. No interest would be compromised. No one would lose anything by refraining from hostilities. Simply standing still, he hoped, would let fears dissipate as their objects did not materialize. Calm contemplation of concrete interests would overcome passions about conflicting abstract visions. But the reverse happened. As Lincoln said: "And the war came."

Lincoln's own commitment to peace through adherence to law is the thread that runs through his war policy. Thus, the First Inaugural's main point is that there would be peace unless the Southern states made war, and that the federal government's response would be neither less nor more than to "protect and defend the Constitution of the United States." Hence, as Lincoln explained on July 4, the executive's war aim was simply to restore the status quo ante as much as possible: ". . . no different understanding of the powers and duties of the Federal government, relatively to the rights of the states, and the people, under the Constitution, than that expressed in the *Inaugural Address*." There would not be "any coercion, any conquest, any subjugation in any just sense of these terms."[2] Because secession was impossible constitutionally, Lincoln argued, the Southern states had never left, and hence their representatives' seats in the Senate and House were there for them to fill at any time. Restoring the Union would be simple. Mere peace would do it.

The Logic of War

War, however, has its own dynamic and logic, destructive and despotic. On May 25, 1836, John Quincy Adams had first warned Southerners to treasure peace because, should their states become theaters of war, the law of war would invest the belligerents with the power to end slavery: "From the instant that your slave holding States become the Theater of war, civil, servile, or foreign, from that instant the war powers of Congress extend to interference with the institution of slavery in every way in which it can be interfered with, from a claim of indemnity for slaves taken or destroyed, to the cession of the State burdened with slavery to a foreign power."[3] That is because *war necessarily follows the logic of victory—absolutely and despotically.*

The US Civil War, like others, made demands on the belligerents, demands that changed their plans. In Lincoln's words, "Neither party expected for the war, the magnitude, or the duration which it has already attained. Neither anticipated that the *cause* of the conflict might cease with, or even before the conflict itself should cease." Defeating formidable Southern armies had required not just terrible attrition in battle but also dislocation of their rear areas by occupation and by promising to emancipate the slaves. There was no question of Lincoln's authority as commander of armies in combat to do whatever might be necessary to their success.

Lincoln's *Emancipation Proclamation*, issued on January 1, 1863, applied to areas under Confederate control. It would expire at the end of the war. He followed the proclamation with a proposal to Congress for emancipating the slaves permanently, through compensation of their owners. But Boston abolitionist William Lloyd Garrison called Lincoln's proposal "demented." The Republicans who controlled Congress thought so, too. Nevertheless, there could be no question, post-war, of reinstating precisely the chief bone of contention that had led to the war. So, by March 1865 much of the South was effectively occupied by an enemy army that was enforcing a socioeconomic revolution—not the peace that Lincoln had in mind.

Nevertheless, Lincoln sought to bring about as much of that peace as he could. Like Washington, he knew that victory consisted not in the hostile army's surrender, but, rather, in renewing friendship between people who had been killing one another for half a decade and thinking about it for a generation before that. The tools available to achieve such a victory are far less tangible, have far less predictable effects, than the ones for crushing armies.

Theodore Roosevelt might have said that Lincoln, having wielded a big stick, would now speak softly. In Winston Churchill's terms, Lincoln's policy was "in victory, magnanimity, in peace, good will."

The Logic of Peace

The Second Inaugural is the most concise evidence of what Lincoln considered his tools and of how he planned to use them. He spoke of the war as a divine "woe to those by whom the offense came."

Lincoln imputes that offense, slavery, to both North and South, since the wealth that came from "the bond-man's . . . unrequited toil" was "piled up" in all parts of the country. Speaking as the spiritual as well as temporal leader of the whole American people, Lincoln asks all to submit to God's punishment, "true and righteous altogether."

And then, in words immortal, Lincoln ends: ". . . with malice toward none; with charity for all; with firmness in the right, as God gives us to see the right, let us strive on to finish the work we are in; to bind up the nation's wounds; to care for him who shall have born the battle, and for his widow and his orphan, to do all which may achieve and cherish a just, and a lasting peace, among ourselves, and with all nations."

The wounds, the battle-worn, the widows and the orphans were those of North and South alike, as is the peace that Lincoln wanted for them.

Nobody got that peace because, upon Lincoln's death, the Republican Party inflicted twelve years of attempted nation-building on Southern states—sucking their remaining wealth, building political rotten-boroughs to pad its powers in Congress, and rubbing salt into wounds by appointing Negroes to positions with punitive powers over whites. Republicans used Negroes as political pawns, and left the pawns to pay the price. Later, the Democrats did the same thing. The amicable 1865 ceremony at Appomattox notwithstanding, the Civil War's hostilities did not end until federal troops were withdrawn from the South in 1877. They echo among us still.

Some in our time blame Lincoln for not aiming the war (and postwar radical Republicans for not aiming Reconstruction) at achieving socioeconomic equality for Negroes. But any attempt forcibly to change Southern people's habits and attitudes would have ensured that thousands of Southerners would have joined guerrilla units such as General Nathan Bedford Forrest's, that the Civil War would have degenerated into insurgency and counterinsurgency, making impossible any kind of peace in America. The Civil War had made sense, to the extent it did, as the resolution of a set of questions about what kind of peace America could live with.

Thereafter, the South secured itself harshly against a Negro population understandably resentful of its former slavery and unaccustomed to self-discipline. Slowly, it joined the North in renewing American nationalism. North and South, people named avenues, buildings, and parks "Grant-Lee." Some have seen in this an obscene compromise at the black man's expense, even in the emotional embraces of old Union and Confederate soldiers at Gettysburg in 1913, on the bloody days' fiftieth anniversary. But it was such a peace as the circumstances permitted.

12

Peacefully Pregnant

Between the Civil War and the Spanish American War of 1898, America grew in peace and thought little of war. US foreign policy was in the moderate hands of William Seward (1861–69)—Lincoln's secretary of state who strove to imitate John Quincy Adams—as well as of James G. Blaine (1881, 1889–92) who idolized Seward, and of President Grover Cleveland (1885–89, 1893–97) devoted to Washington's ways. They guarded America with a solvent balance between the ends and means of international intercourse. While no nation picked a fight with America, Americans steered clear of others' quarrels. Meanwhile, elements were growing within America's culture that yearned to make great improvements at home and abroad, paid less attention to balancing ends with means, and took peace for granted.

From colonial days, circumstances had forced Americans to pay attention to how peace might be won or lost. The Indians and the French, the overbearing British, the Napoleonic wars, the Civil War that loomed for forty years before it devastated, had made sure that Americans did not take peace for granted. But between 1865 and World War I Americans, especially Northerners, had a hard time believing that they had to think about keeping the peace.

Peace for Granted

"All was agreement of soul with soul"—John Quincy Adams's description of the founding of Plymouth Colony—may well have been William Seward's paradigm of foreign policy: grow America through amicable agreements with foreigners, which reinforce the same at home. Seward invited foreigners to become Americans, and purchased foreign territory. But Seward recoiled from his own project to purchase Santo Domingo for the same reasons that Adams had relegated thoughts about annexing Cuba to the realm of theory: Important though the island is, its people could not be an organic part of the Union. Nor should they be ruled against their consent. By contrast, Seward purchased Alaska with alacrity, because its few civilized residents had the option of becoming Americans or of returning to Russia. Seward also sponsored the Immigration Act of 1864 that paid passage to would-be Americans. He traveled Mexico urging its people to come north. He hoped that whole sections of Canada and Mexico would Americanize and join the US en masse. A devoté of the Monroe Doctrine, Seward prodded France's Napoleon III to abandon his venture in Mexico merely by pointing out its inherent futility and repugnance to the American people, who the French knew were chomping at the bit to evict his forces.

Seward fondly repeated the verse: "Our nation with united interests blest, Not now content to pose, shall sway the rest; Abroad our empire shall no limits know, But like the sea in boundless circles flow." Yet his notion of empire had nothing to do with conquest but rather with boundless commerce on the seven seas. It never contradicted his commitment to voluntarism, which he equated with peace.

All that and good will certainly animated his approach to Asia. Anson Burlingame, Seward's ambassador to China, was so congenial that China named him *its* ambassador to the Western world. Thus the 1868 US-China Treaty was written entirely by Americans. Among its many amicable provisions was unrestricted travel between the two countries. That, however, ended up producing anti-coolie riots in California, and hence friction with China. Similarly, under Seward's tenure, Americans supported Japan's Meiji Restoration and provided the basic instruction in Western ways that raised that country to the ranks of great power. In this case too, Americans' peaceful involvement with a foreign people that they did not fully understand resulted in something other than peace.

James G. Blaine, the era's Mr. Republican, dedicated his stewardship of foreign affairs mostly to brokering peace and cooperation in

Latin America. Whether his efforts did more harm than good is arguable. That is because, while his objectives were the same as Adams's and Seward's, his diplomacy descended more into the substance of the Latin Americans' relations with one another than Blaine's mentors would have counseled.

Blaine spent most of his brief first term as secretary of state trying to mediate an end to the War of the Pacific (1879–83), which pitted Chile against Peru and Bolivia. As happens so often, the mediators took sides or at any rate were seen as doing so. This brought peace no closer, but strained relations between the US and all belligerents. In his second term, Blaine sought to broker peace between Mexico and Guatemala. As should have been expected, the weaker Guatemala tried to use Blaine's diplomacy to make up for some of its battlefield disadvantages, thus souring US-Mexican relations. Nevertheless, Blaine's commitment to hemispheric peace was so strong and sincere that the inter-American conference that he convened grew into the Organization of American States.

How Blaine and his successors dealt with Hawaii illustrates that their intentions remained remarkably constant while changing circumstances were shifting the ground on which they operated. Blaine had learned about Hawaii in the 1840s from his home state of Maine's whalers. By the 1880s Hawaii had been largely Americanized by missionaries as well as by American planters. The royal family lived and dressed in the American style, real power resided in an American-dominated legislature, and US ships well-nigh monopolized the magnificent Pearl Harbor. The US government's position on the islands had not changed: They should remain independent but, because of their geographic position, they must not be possessed by anyone hostile to the United States under any circumstances. Blaine upheld that position until his death in January 1893.

That very month, however, Hawaii's queen Liliuokalani tried to take back the legislature's powers. The local Americans deposed her with the help of Marines from the USS *Boston,* and asked Washington for annexation. But the incoming President Grover Cleveland refused to submit the treaty to the Senate. The annexation of Hawaii happened only during the Spanish American War, justified as a military necessity.

Flexing Muscles

Yet the same Grover Cleveland, so scrupulous of peace that he refused Hawaii, came close to making war on Great Britain in 1895 merely because the British had refused highhandedly a US suggestion that it submit a border dispute with Venezuela to arbitration. For the occasion, Secretary of State Richard Olney unveiled a new version of the Monroe Doctrine: "Today the United States is practically sovereign on this continent and its fiat is law upon the subjects to which it confines its interposition. . . . Its infinite resources combined with its isolated position render it master of the situation and practically invulnerable as against any or all other powers."[1] Cleveland loved Olney's dictum, and convened a special session of Congress to provide for whatever means might be necessary to enforce it. Why? Because the American people reacted to Britain's slight as if they had been waiting for a chance to throw America's great and growing weight around. In a sense, they had—but still without taste for empire.

The ambiguous attitude of conservative Americans may be seen from the fact that, a half-decade later, the same Olney and Cleveland who had threatened to make war on very-great-power Great Britain opposed acquiring the Philippines from prostrated Spain. Why? In 1900, Olney wrote: "[No great power] can afford not to make the welfare of its own people its primary object—none can afford to regard itself as a sort of missionary nation charged with the rectification of wrongs the world over. Were the United States to enter upon its new international role with the serious purpose of carrying out any such theory, it would not merely be laughed at but voted a nuisance by all other nations—and treated accordingly."[2]

These warnings fell on deaf ears, because people who see themselves as benefactors, harbingers of peace, cannot imagine that others would find them insufferable.

Dreaming of Great Things

The most consequential aspect of this period's history is the multiplicity of ways in which the American people's ebullience overshadowed their commitment to peace.

The intellectual strands come together in the most popular book of the 1880s, Josiah Strong's *Our Country*. The book is a detailed catalogue of the United States' enormous productivity, wealth, and miraculous growth, as well as of the problems inherent in that growth: urbanization, the abuse of alcohol and tobacco, the perils of excessive wealth, unrestricted immigration, Roman Catholicism, etc. But every page is permeated by the sense that the United States is God's, and Charles Darwin's, designee for perfection and for dominance of the planet. Racial and cultural determinism, pride in piety and in freedom, combine with patriotism to produce a sense of duty to improve our country and through it all mankind "Till the war-drum throbs no longer and the battle flags are furl'd, In the Parliament of Man, the Federation of the World."

Americans, already the most numerous of the Anglo-Saxon race, were molding immigrants from many nations effectively into that race, superior in clean, humane, productive habits, in "the purest Christianity, the widest possible civil liberty."[3] Because nature commands the supremacy of the fittest, Americans' very superiority will lead and evangelize the world without firing a shot.

Our Country was so popular because the capacity to do great things—and the illusion that they could be done without breaking a sweat—was so sweet to so many.

In the year of its publication (1885) Woodrow Wilson published his major work, *Congressional Government: A Study in American Politics,* which argued explicitly that America's founders had done the country and the world a disservice by crafting a Constitution that makes it difficult for the government to do great things at home and abroad. Neither book, nor any other major work of the time, considers what means would be required to achieve any given Great Thing, or whose peace might be upset thereby.

Both celebrated America's wondrous strength. Both dealt abstractly with using that strength for the greater good in all matters, including military ones. But, unlike Pericles, both authors seem unconscious that this strength rests on a precarious balance.

From the twenty-first century's vantage point, it is all too easy to see here the embryos of wars waged at home for perfecting Americans:

Prohibition, eugenics, and various forms of political correctness, as well as "nation-building" abroad and at home.

Feeling greatness coursing through their veins, the American people took increasing interest in military matters, or at least in naval ones. Alfred Thayer Mahan's *The Influence of Sea Power upon History: 1660–1783* (1890) led many Americans to reflect on how much their security depends on control of the seas, to realize that America did not exercise that control, and to consider what it would take to control its seaward approaches: uniting the Atlantic and Pacific coasts through an Isthmian canal, as well as building a merchant marine and a navy. A historian, Mahan did not advocate throwing America's weight around. Nor were his many enthusiasts warmongers. Indeed, the intra-American conversation on naval matters in the 1890s was strictly about defending the world's newest great power.

13

Empire?

At the turn of the twentieth century, while most Americans remained devoted to peace and averse to empire, America went to war and acquired an empire. The dissonance arose because many statesmen on all sides of the issues of the time did not think through how their preferences affected the peace that all cherished. As events forced them to clarify their own priorities, the issue of empire disappeared more quickly than it had arisen, while a profound and lasting division over the meaning of peace developed.

The American people did not declare war on Spain in 1898 to take over its empire. Rather, the press and the pulpit thundered against the cruelties that Spain was inflicting on Cubans "practically on our doorstep." Did not Americans have the duty to stop them? So what if this was someone else's business? If the Good Samaritan had turned the corner on the road to Jericho as the proverbial mugging was being committed, would he not have stopped it? So what if Jesus had not told the parable that way? Why should not America use its power to do good?

The motives for intervention in Cuba were certifiably clean and benevolent: Before the declaration of war had come to a vote, the Foraker Amendment had forsworn any intention of annexing the island. And the Philippines? Well, they just happened to come into America's possession. Should the Filipinos be cast adrift in their miserable condition? President William McKinley had agonized and concluded that since they were humans "for whom Christ also died," America should take care of them.

No More Empire

But the lighthearted popular consensus for empire stopped there. Was it possible peaceably to uplift the Filipinos? Most thought not. Nor could Americans imagine Filipinos as fellow citizens. Opposition to annexation was so strong that the Senate approved it by only two votes, and only because of partisan calculations that had nothing to do with the issue. The Supreme Court's judgment on the matter, in "The Insular Cases," evaded the essential questions and was embarrassing to those who wrote it as to those who read it.

The political struggle, however, showed that a sector of American opinion had drifted far from the founders' priorities. Senator Albert Beveridge (R-IN) stated the extreme imperialist position: "self-government and internal development have been the dominant notes of our first century; administration and the development of other lands will be the dominant notes of our second century." To impose American rule on others is not to deny them liberty, because we know what liberty is, and they do not. Does such imposition violate something fundamental about America? No: "The Declaration of Independence does not forbid us to do our part in the regeneration of the world. If it did, the Declaration would be wrong."[1] So much for piety toward America's foundations.

Few people, however, shared a commitment to ruling foreigners so deep and strong as explicitly to override the Republic's explicit tenets. Even Beveridge was not looking forward to constant colonial warfare. None wanted confrontations with great powers. America's turn of the century imperialists were not "the family of the lion or the tribe of the eagle" that Lincoln feared. Far from being Caesars or Napoleons, they imagined short, glorious little wars against retrograde bad guys, followed by decades during which they would peacefully enjoy the pleasures of Sahibs among grateful subjects—identities and illusions they share with their successors in our time.

But the war that the US government waged against the Philippine independence movement between 1899 and 1903 was almost as cruel as Spain's in Cuba. Reports that US troops were inflicting what would later be called "water-boarding" on the natives shook the

body politic and damped ardor for repeating the experience any-
where else. Andrew Carnegie's quip that in the course of building a
heaven on earth for the Filipinos the US government had sent thousands of them to heaven directly resonated with the public. That
included Theodore Roosevelt and Henry Cabot Lodge, who had
been among the foremost advocates of American empire.

The unpleasantness of the Philippine insurrection merely recon-
firmed long-standing American attitudes about foreign affairs. As
late as 1884 public opinion had considered it perilous, immoral,
and un-American for President Chester Arthur's envoy to the Berlin
conference that delineated the Belgian Congo from French, British,
and Portuguese colonies to have signed the final document *even as
a mere observer.* Yet in 1899 a generation of American statesmen
eagerly signed on to the latest version of European imperialism. The
bard of the British Empire, Rudyard Kipling, welcomed them with
his poem "The White Man's Burden." It sang not of glory, but of
duty—thankless and perhaps senseless:

> *Take up the White Man's burden—*
> *Send forth the best ye breed—*
> *Go bind your sons to exile*
> *To serve your captives' need;*
> *To wait in heavy harness,*
> *On fluttered folk and wild—*
> *Your new-caught, sullen peoples,*
> *Half-devil and half-child.*[2]

This sort of thing had little appeal even for jingoistic Americans,
never mind for the rest. The imperialists had managed only a short-
term seduction.

So by 1905 imperialism was a dead issue: Ardent anti-imperialists
agreed that the Panama Canal zone was an extension of the US
coastline, and that Hawaii and Puerto Rico were outworks for continental defense. They were satisfied that Puerto Ricans could become
independent any time they wanted, and that Filipinos would be given
independence whether they liked it or not as soon as it was prudent

to give it. But no imperialist advocated any more Philippines, ever. That looked like an ex post facto victory in public opinion for the anti-imperialists' vision of peace. At best it was victory by default.

While the imperialists had recoiled at the most visible, unpleasant, expensive consequences of the Philippine occupation, they never took to heart their opponents' fundamental arguments. Neither Beveridge nor pro-empire academics such as Woodrow Wilson ever dealt with the charge that occupying foreign countries meant upsetting the American republic's own delicate balance of habits, virtues, and vices. Nor did they ask themselves whether America's occupation of one Asian country might portend war with or involvement in the quarrels of other Asian powers.

The Deeper Division

Significantly for the long run, the advocates of empire succeeded in branding their opponents as "isolationists" who stood in the way of America's greatness, of presence in the four corners of the world, and of an undefined duty to improve it—things that, expressed in generalities, well nigh everyone wanted.

But few advocates and opponents of empire alike addressed the larger issue of what America's role as one of the world's preeminent powers ought to be. How does the world's largest industrial and agricultural producer, a country so big and energetic that its ships and people penetrate all continents, whose power every foreign state and faction thereof yearns to bring to bear on its own quarrels for its own purposes, manage to keep George Washington's "peace and friendship" with all? What *is* to be great-power America's peace, and how is it to be secured?

Imperialists and anti-imperialists merely confided in America's own peaceful, inoffensive motives and ways. Most on all sides agreed that since America would provoke no one, attack no one, deal fairly with all, no foreigner would pick a fight with the American colossus.

The anti-imperialist argument that mere possession of territory in Asia meant involvement in Asian quarrels was too abstract to compel many people to ponder how others might react to America's presence in their neighborhood. No one wanted to *interfere* in others' affairs. Yet all agreed that Americans would lead all along the paths of progress. Few asked why foreigners would not judge such leadership to be unacceptable interference.

The division over empire had masked a deeper division that would endure over the next century, and that redefined the identity of some of America's leading figures. To wit, in 1898–1901 Theodore Roosevelt and Henry Cabot Lodge were the best-known and most powerful advocates for America's *aggrandizement abroad*. For the rest of their lives, both retained their views of that time. Nevertheless, Lodge (and hence Roosevelt, had he lived) went down in history as the arch *isolationist* because he led opposition to US entry into the League of Nations. Historians have not had the courage to pin the *isolationist* label on Albert Beveridge, whom they cannot help but use as the premier *imperialist,* but who ended up opposing the League more vehemently than Lodge. Moreover, Roosevelt and Lodge lived and died as advocates of US military power, whereas self-proclaimed internationalists usually coupled grandiose ends with the *reduction* of US power.

In a nutshell, the enduring divide ended up being not between imperialists and anti-imperialists, but between self-proclaimed "internationalists"—who identified America's interests with mankind's, but did not deem it necessary to match commitment to world reform with the power to effect it—and those who calibrated America's national interest with the means for pursuing it. All aimed, hoped, expected that America would live in peace. Historians' labeling of the latter as *isolationists* obscures the true nature of what divided and continues to divide Americans.

≪ 14 ≫

Nation, or World?

After the 1904 election, as statesmen came to grips with the differences that underlay the superficial consensus on peace, progress, and American greatness, the new camps into which they sorted themselves included former advocates and opponents of empire. One of these camps, whose intellectual leadership came from the presidents of Columbia, Stanford, and Princeton universities (Nicholas Murray Butler, David Starr Jordan, and Woodrow Wilson) and included such statesmen as Elihu Root and industrialist Andrew Carnegie, wanted America to lead the world in establishing "mechanisms of peace" and progress—meaning networks of international commitments to settle the world's quarrels—while transcending alliances and military force. Its occupants thought that this was possible, because mankind's desire for peace was already there, just covered up by an antiquated international system. Clear that away, and world peace would blossom.

The other camp, led by Theodore Roosevelt and Henry Cabot Lodge, focused on promoting America's interests as a great power among great powers. For them, America's peace would result from making limited commitments on its own behalf, backed by military power.

The former camp prevailed. By the time the Great War struck, America's public discourse was dominated by a concept of peace impossible to realize, the corruption of which yet pollutes American statecraft in our time.

Theodore Roosevelt, Ends and Means

In 1897 Roosevelt had pointed to those who "protest against a navy and protest also against every movement to carry out the traditional policy of the country in foreign affairs." He called them "doctrinaires whose eyes are so firmly fixed on the golden vision of universal peace that they cannot see the grim facts of real life . . . [who] prate about love for mankind, or for another country as being in some hidden way a substitute for love of their own country."[1] Roosevelt was harshest against those who wanted America to take on greater international responsibilities but opposed matching commitments with military power. He compared those who had favored taking the Philippines, but who now refused to modernize and expand the US Navy to Presidents Jefferson and Madison, whose failure to support their remonstrance against Britain with a strong navy had brought on the War of 1812.

Placing American troops in the Philippines without the backing of a strong US Navy, Roosevelt charged, invited war with Japan. If Americans want peace in the Pacific, he said, either withdraw from the Philippines or build a navy that Japan must respect.

Roosevelt simply reaffirmed the maxim that peace depends on the proper balance between commitments and the capacity to uphold them. His handling of the Russo-Japanese war of 1905 illustrated what he meant by the need to "speak softly." America's interest in the Pacific Rim was best served by a balance between the region's several powers, especially Russia and Japan. Thus, it was in America's interest that the war between the two come to an end with as little lingering acrimony as possible. In pursuing this interest, the United States could no more afford to be seen as diplomatically partial to either side than it could to take sides militarily. Hence Roosevelt mediated peace between the two with the lightest possible hand, not suggesting any particular solution, never mind guaranteeing any result.

The eventual settlement between the parties ended up slightly more generous to Russia than battlefield results might have suggested. Anti-American riots ensued in Tokyo. Roosevelt acknowledged that his mediation had touched the limit of what is proper in one nation's involvement in others' affairs. The few mild words that he had spoken in pursuit of a peace marginal to US interests had almost triggered a direct threat to America's own peace. The point is that the balance between commitments and power is inherently tenuous.

Though Roosevelt shared the expansive sentiments of the age, he never lost his grip on the fact that the statesman's good will is less important for the production of peace than is tight, jealous weighing of particular interests, animosities, vulnerabilities against what any and all can bring to bear on the situation.

In the end, the spirit of the age triumphed over most of Roosevelt's contemporaries, and their progeny.

Elihu Root

None embodied that spirit more than Elihu Root, Theodore Roosevelt's secretary of war and then of state. Root, arguably the fountainhead-mentor of twentieth-century American statesmen, helped teach a generation that America must lead the world to a new and better kind of international relations, in which reason and persuasion would replace force. In 1907 he announced that the US government would no longer put its power behind the collection of private debts in Latin America, no matter how legitimate, thereby hoping to teach the world to bend over backwards not to give injury, not to insult. He believed that this would increase respect for America. Root had supported the acquisition of the Philippines in part because by it America could show the world a new kind of stewardship. He was more responsible than anyone for the Hague conference of 1907 that sought to set bounds to the rigors of war as well as for the later conference that established the International Court of Justice, for which he was awarded the Nobel Peace Prize for 1912.

As Root explained in his acceptance speech, "pulling up the roots" of war means building impartial tribunals to settle controversies. Doing this promotes good habits and is contagious. Nations can make treaty commitments to be bound by arbitration. International law consists of commitments. Root saw the Hague conference of 1907 as a body that makes international law, a code that comes to exist somehow over and above individual treaties. How? Because modern economic well-being requires peace and order. Governments abide by international law because it is profitable to do so, and because people must surely force governments to do only what is profitable and honorable.

Increasingly educated, sophisticated peoples will support only their governments' just demands: "[F]irst, there has come to be a public opinion of the world; second, that opinion has set up a new standard of international conduct which condemns unjustified aggression; and third the public opinion of the world punishes the violation of its standard. . . . The spread of education, the enormous increase in the production and distribution of newspapers . . . the telegraph . . . the new mobility of mankind . . . travel by steamship and railroad . . . the vast extension of international commerce, [the nations'] dependence on each other for the supply of their needs . . ." will make sure that the peoples will push for peaceful, rational international relations. Morality, as well as "economic science," demands it. Hence "must" equals "will." "When any people feels that its government has done a shameful thing and has brought them into disgrace in the opinion of the world, theirs will be the vengeance and they will inflict the punishment."[2]

Root persuaded President William Howard Taft to negotiate compulsory bilateral arbitration treaties with a number of countries. The Senate rejected the idea, prompting Root and the scheme's partisans to blame America in general and their political opponents in particular for standing in the way of progress.

Nicholas Murray Butler

According to Columbia's Nicholas Murray Butler, new diplomatic "mechanisms" can transform the world. Such "mechanisms" are networks of mutual commitments, to which the nations must abide because,

> To suppose that men and women into whose intellectual and moral instruction and upbuilding have gone the glories of the world's philosophy and art and poetry and religion, into whose lives have

been poured for two thousand years the precepts and the inspiration of the Christian religion, over whose daily conduct have been thrown since the days of Draco and of Solon the restraints of law and of consideration for the rights and property of others—to suppose that these men and women when gathered together in groups called nations . . . are to fly at each others' throats to burn, to ravage, to kill, in the hope of somehow establishing thereby truth and right and justice is to suppose the universe to be stood upon its apex. . . .[3]

The world, said Butler, has become one big neighborhood, and the family of mankind, once a theoretical notion, has become a practical fact. Today (1907) we have dealings with folks in Bombay more easily than we used to have with a neighboring village. What will force nations to abide by the judgments of international bodies? The people will force them, because they would be ashamed not to.

It was characteristic of this generation's Progressives that, although they thought America uniquely qualified to lead mankind forward, they—on principle—considered America morally and politically on a par with the rest of mankind. In this they differed radically from America's founders, who saw America as unique because of its people's commitment to live by superior principles. Indeed, turn-of-the-century Progressives were eager to prove their equanimity by criticizing America (or Britain) as readily or more readily than other nations. After all, when those who should lead by example fail to do so, they prove themselves *worse* than those who do not follow good example because none is given. If it were possible to indict a whole nation, Butler wrote in 1907, Britain should be put in the dock because of its fixation on Dreadnought class battleships. What right have the British to criticize Germany's naval plans? Does only Britain have the right to a big navy? Is it mere jealousy because of Germany's advances in science, industry, and sanitation? *All* navies are a bane on the world. And it is high time that the United States, too, reduce its naval building program, for it is inherently no less warlike than anyone else's.

Strongly did Butler disbelieve in the coming of the Great War. Yet, when it came, his and his fellows' enthusiasm for their views only increased. In July 1918 Butler wrote that the war had made necessary the ultimate "mechanism": a League of Nations.

In 1925 Butler replaced Root at the head of the Carnegie Endowment for International Peace. Under him its scholars, alongside their counterparts from other countries, would develop the knowledge necessary to build even better mechanisms.

David Starr Jordan

For Stanford's David Starr Jordan, America was special, because the American people's geographic freedom of action and their lack of historical burdens gave them greater opportunities for becoming a moral cut above others. Hence Americans should be proud of their peaceful relations with their neighbors to the North, ashamed of their transgressions toward those to the South, and even more ashamed of succumbing to the common passions of mankind, such as armaments, liquor, and tobacco. In his most popular work, *The Blood of the Nation: A Study of the Decay of Races through the Survival of the Unfit* (1902), he proposed eugenically refining the American people to lead the world.

"There is nothing in the world for us to fight for," wrote this stern moral teacher, "at least not with sword and gun. Waste and greed and folly must be fought, but against these we need better weapons. . . . We do not need [battleships]. There are no enemies against which we could use them, no friends which [*sic*] we could even for that purpose turn into enemies. The war scares with Germany and Japan are made up for a purpose by foolish and wicked men . . . to exploit these scares is a crime against decency. . . ." Jordan counseled leading America to "free the world." How? "We will leave all disputes to the decision of a tribunal of just men. The word war shall be erased from our national speech."[4] Jordan wrote: "the motto of the cosmopolitan clubs of our universities made up of men of all races" is "above all, humanity!"[5]

Because he could not imagine that the world was not faculty clubs and conferences writ large, he was certain that only a few evil men stood between humanity and its natural state of peace.

Woodrow Wilson

Woodrow Wilson synthesized Root's faith in humanity, Butler's faith in organizational schemes, and Jordan's disdain for the evils of traditional international relations as well as passion for forceful reformation. He advanced the notion that America's mission is to bring peace and unity to mankind. He did so in a way that accused disbelievers of being in league with the Devil. Reality just had to bend to his superior morality; *and to the extent it did not, his domestic political opponents must bear the blame.* The practice of indicting domestic political-social opponents for the fact that reality did not bend to his wishes proved profitable, but brought home to America some of the strife that it inflicted on the world. It is with us still.

Even after the Great War had shown the futility of arbitration treaties as a solution to the word's problems, Wilson continued pushing for them. This in *October, 1914:*

> The sum and substance of these treaties is that whenever trouble arises the light shall shine on it for a year before anything is done; and my prediction is that after the light has shone on it a year it will not be necessary to do any thing; that after we know what happened, then we will know who was right and who was wrong.[6]

As the war's violence worsened under the lash of enraged public opinion in all belligerent countries, Wilson began to preach democratic self-determination as the permanent solution to the violence— gasoline as the remedy for fire.

Wilson first pretended even-handedness toward the belligerents, but ended up describing Germany's system of government as the last remaining barrier to the achievement of the Progressives' Nirvana. In Wilson's declamations, mankind was always just one enemy's elimination away from perpetual peace. When Germany's monarchy went away, the last enemy became armaments, or a kind of diplomacy. Then it was US Republicans. Surely, it was booze. Eliminate the object of his obloquy, and the world would be reborn.

Instead of trying to explain how and why the lifting of this or that burden would cause universal peace to spring forth, Wilson wove a tapestry of fantasies out of high-sounding words. America's aim, said his war message of April 2, 1917, was "to set up amongst the really free and self-governed peoples of the world . . . a concert of purpose and of action." Who these "really free" peoples were he never said. Nor was there ever the slightest reason to believe that an international concert of purposes existed. The message put great stock on "the organized opinion of mankind." That did not exist, and has not existed since.

The vacuity of Wilson's language was not lost on his contemporaries. In March 1915, *The New Republic* wrote:

> It is the quality of Mr. Wilson's thinking to make even the most concrete things seem like abstractions. . . . When you have purged and bleached your morality into a collection of abstract nouns, you have something that is clean and white, but what else have you? Surely nothing comparable to the usefulness of that wisdom that retains the odor of the world . . . mankind cannot live by golden affirmations. . . .

Wilson's loose lips sank more than ships. He brokered the surrender of Germany on the basis of false promises of equal treatment—of a peace settlement in which the only winner would be mankind. But his intervention made the Versailles Treaty a mess that failed to protect the winners, outraged the losers, and failed to satisfy the expectations Wilson had raised. Wilson maintained the blockade on Germany for eight moths after the armistice, while Allied armies removed Germany's remaining food stocks. Hundreds of thousands starved, and murderous hate stored up. Since Wilson projected the image of America as the deliverer of each belligerent's dearest objectives, and because he was unable to deliver any of them, he displeased all in America's name.

Each and every one of the creatures that Wilson conceived at Versailles, from the special status of the Rhineland and the Polish Corridor to Yugoslavia, to Czechoslovakia, to the Mandates of Palestine, Syria, and Iraq, ended up as the proximate cause of one or more wars—horrors for which America bears some responsibility. Particularly gratuitous and fateful was Wilson's alienation of Japan, whose good relationship with Britain he destroyed.

His effects on America's internal peace were worse. America, he said, had "no reason for being" except to "stand for the rights of men," to be "champions of humanity," whatever that meant. *No* reason for being? But pursuing America's reason for being as Wilson defined it had meant the death of 117,000 young Americans on the Western front in a year and a half. For what, their fellow citizens asked? They concluded: "Never again!" Americans also choked on the illogic of Wilson's international scheme: The League could not oblige all nations to go to war for each and each to go to war for all, and at the same time relieve each and all of the need ever to go to war. Wilson's Great War had brought the deadly flu of 1918. Wilson's other legacy, Prohibition, started a shooting war at home.

Wilson, moved by a vision, sowed the wind and left others to reap the whirlwind. Like so may who did that, he got the Nobel Peace Prize.

The American people rejected Wilson's party in the election of 1920. But, because Wilson's progressivism had become orthodoxy among America's best and brightest of both parties, logic and elections proved weak against it. For both parties, peace had come to mean not the sober balance of ends and means, but a pacifism as mindless as it was frenetic and provocative. Wilson's presidency also gave birth to a more-or-less united ruling class intoxicated with its own virtue and ideology, increasingly divorced from public opinion which struggled to keep a grip on common sense.

15

Pacifism vs. Peace

The Great War's outcome convinced most Americans correctly that they had been misled into meaningless slaughter—incorrectly that statecraft means war, and hence that peace means not even contemplating the use of military force. Mindless pacifism obscured the memory of statesmen from Washington to Theodore Roosevelt who had calibrated commitments and resources to preserve peace or to reestablish it. In 1914 Roosevelt had argued that throwing America's diplomatic weight onto Britain's side would restrain Germany from attacking France through the Low Countries and hence from triggering the Great War. But President Wilson, in the name of peace and neutrality, had refused to make a commitment that stood a chance of actually preserving peace. He eschewed concrete proposals in favor of gauzy language, on the basis of which he plunged America into endless commitments and a century of war.

Roosevelt died in 1919. By that year American elites of both parties had abandoned the notion of keeping the peace through statesmanship in favor of demonstrations and declarations of love for peace and of hate for anything having to do with war. Thus they banished thought of how peace might be secured. We now ponder how the pacifism of the ensuing decades vitiated peace.

Rejection of traditional statecraft was the common denominator of the Interwar Years' many strains of pacifism.

All Together

Democrat Wilson's project for a League of Nations was a variant of a proposal, the "League to Enforce Peace," developed in April 1915 by Republicans: former President William Howard Taft, future President Herbert Hoover, and near-President Charles Evans Hughes. Countries would agree to submit disputes to arbitration, as well as to gang up militarily on any that reneged. In 1919, some Republican members of the US League, notably Root and Hughes, balked when faced with the practical commitment to automatically go to war that was the heart of Wilson's League of Nations. Others, like Democrat Franklin Roosevelt, had second thoughts when faced with the League's unpopularity.

Organizational matters aside, the views of all the above-mentioned internationalists on the substance of foreign affairs were remarkably parallel with those of the Versailles Treaty's most extreme opponents, like William Borah and Gerald P. Nye. As regards peace, there was little daylight between all these and America's elite in business and law, the likes of Thomas Watson of IBM and Thomas Lamont of J. P. Morgan, Bernard Baruch, and Henry Morgenthau, as well as America's most prominent Protestant layman, John Foster Dulles of the New York law firm Sullivan and Cromwell, who had been Wilson's student at Princeton and had worked for him at Versailles: They were all for it, emphatically. Details be damned.

The insubstantial substance of this vast pacifist consensus may be seen in the near-universal praise visited upon Secretary of State Charles Evans Hughes's proposal of the 1921 Washington Naval Treaty, and regarding East Asia.

Wilson had tried to square the League's guarantee of peace with the obligation to defend it by saying that the obligation was only "moral." Senator Warren Harding had shown Wilson's vacuity: "If that be true and any nation may put aside or exercise its judgment as to the moral obligation . . . what do we get out of this international compact in the enforcement of any decree?"[1] Harding was elected president in 1920 in part for having pointed out that peace would have to be earned the old-fashioned way. But President Harding had made Hughes secretary of state.

The Washington Treaties of 1921

Hughes showed how thoroughly the bipartisan ruling class shared Wilson's intellectual premises. Hughes became a hero to millions, because his proposal to fix the ratio of the world's main battleship fleets required scrapping more warship tonnage than had been sunk in all the world's naval wars combined. Hughes also gathered the signatures to the Nine Power Treaty, a commitment (principally by the United States and Japan) to one of America's perennial objectives— the independence, territorial integrity, and equal access to China, the "Open Door." Hughes also substituted an alliance among the United States, Britain, France, and Japan, obviously directed at no one, for the Anglo–Japanese alliance that anti-Japanese elements in Asia had feared. By embracing Hughes's proposals, America's elites wedded pacifism to universal commitment, without realizing that these are incompatible.

A few pointed out that the naval agreement let all the powers keep new construction, that most of the vessels scrapped would have been anyway, that the agreement barely restricted aircraft carriers and did not mention other classes of ships. Moreover, if geography were taken into account, the ratios disadvantaged bicoastal America and France, and multicommitted Britain vis-à-vis Asia-centered Japan. Most of all, the price Japan had exacted for agreeing to the ratio— the non-fortification of American bases in the Philippines and above all in Guam—excluded faraway America from naval power in the Western Pacific and guaranteed Japan a free hand in Asia. Given that, the nine-power commitment to the Open Door was worse than meaningless. It was deceptive. Moreover, Japan would regard Hughes's substitution of the Four Power Pact for the Anglo-Japanese alliance as a racial insult.

America's best and brightest found such details offensive: They *knew* that wars are caused by fear and misunderstanding feeding on themselves, that weapons cause fear, and that removing weapons would turn the cycle of war-causality in the opposite direction. Mutual willingness to limit battleships had to carry over to other armaments and to all international relations. By leading the way to restraint, by showing that its chief interest was mankind's common interest in peace, America was surely gaining diplomatic credit. Why fortify Guam? Why place in Japanese hearts something that they would reasonably regard as a thorn? But how unreasonable it was for Japan to resent American pressure on Britain to withdraw from the Anglo-Japanese alliance!

Alas, Japan was not interested in aimless amicability, but in the satisfaction of its needs in Asia. In the name of peace and of commitment to China's integrity, American statesmen opposed satisfying those needs. But they gave no thought to what upholding that integrity would entail. Few noticed the contradiction between committing to China while, in the name of peace, divesting America of the capacity to protect it. Meanwhile, by granting Japan naval superiority over the Western Pacific Rim, Americans made it possible for Japan to satisfy those needs through war. Because no one, least of all Americans, would uphold the nine-power treaty, America was practicing what Theodore Roosevelt had called "peace with insult," combining *"the unbridled tongue with the unready hand."*

Herbert Hoover

The test came when Japan invaded Northern China on September 18, 1931. A predictable pattern followed. Secretary of State Henry L. Stimson noted in his diary that this was "a flagrant violation of the spirit and probably the letter of all the treaties." He brought the matter to President Herbert Hoover, who told him that Japan's primary violation was of its general commitment to the League of Nations (not to the specifics of the nine-power treaty that America had sponsored). Said Hoover, the League must not be allowed to deposit the matter on America's doorstep, because America must not be put in "a humiliating position, in case Japan refused to do anything about what he called our scraps of paper or paper treaties." Stimson's diary continued: "We have nothing but scraps of paper . . . and if we lie down and treat [treaties] like scraps of paper . . . the peace movement will receive a blow that it will not recover from for a long time."[2]

Nevertheless, Hoover and Stimson answered Japan's reneging on its commitment to China's integrity under the nine-power treaty (as well as to peace under the League treaty) by neither upholding its commitment to China nor renouncing it, neither fortifying Guam and the Philippines nor abandoning them, but merely by notifying Japan and China *equally* that the United States would not recognize changes in borders brought about by violence.

Thus Hoover and Stimson "punted," because they refused to take responsibility for either of the real alternatives, both of which showed how foolish were their principles and how mistaken their policies. But they considered their pretense as "reinforcing the treaty structure, particularly the Kellogg-Briand Pact" that had outlawed war.

The Kellogg Pact of 1927's loud but abstract affirmation of the post-1919 peace forevermore veiled the signers' concrete determination not to defend that peace. A textbook example of pacifism, the pact required nothing of its supporters while giving them a claim of moral superiority over their domestic political adversaries. Internationally, it signaled that the signers would not defend the peace. Domestically, it added fuel to partisan strife.

More Pacifist Than Thou

Who abhorred war the most was America's main foreign policy issue of the 1920s. Senator William Borah (R-ID), in the history books as an isolationist, campaigned tirelessly for outlawing war—a universal commitment. Like other Progressives, he believed that all peoples are equally peaceful. So, there would be no need to enforce the commitment. He believed that arms cause wars. Hence he pled for America's disarmament while accusing his opponents of being warmongers. Terribly convenient for himself.

In 1924 Borah accused Robert Lansing, who had been Wilson's secretary of state, of insufficient fidelity to his chief: "'Peoples do not make war' declared Mr. Lansing's great leader. The peoples of the different nations were not responsible for the late war." Hence, "If we are to end war, we must get back of governments and diplomats and ex secretaries, back of leagues and courts, to that educated, aroused, and well directed public opinion. . . ." "Neither can we wait, nor need we wait until all questions about which nations may hold differing views are settled before we begin to limit our armament expenditures." To consider the substance of quarrels rather than to rid one's self of the deadly means of waging them "is to declare in another way that we propose to settle these questions ultimately by force. . . ." "For myself," he concluded, "I refuse to concede that force is the only power left. . . . It cannot be possible."

Borah topped off his demonstration of his own righteousness with a plea for what became the Kellogg-Briand Treaty. He channeled the Gospel: "Is it not time to lay the ax at the root of the tree, to recognize war no longer as legitimate, to declare nations and men criminals who engage in this supercrime?"[3] Woodrow Wilson had legitimized the use of hyperbolic language about war and peace. Politicians found it personally useful to state lofty goals while avoiding concrete language for which they might be held responsible.

Republican President Herbert Hoover, star of David Starr Jordan's first graduating class at Stanford, more pacifist, more progressive than the Wilsonians, was arguably the greatest supporter of Kellogg-Briand. In 1929 Hoover said of Kellogg-Briand: "There is no more significant step in this progress than the solemn covenant that civilized nations have now entered, to renounce war and to settle disputes by pacific means. It is this realignment of the mind of the world that gives the hope of peace." He argued that Wilson's idea of the League had straddled the issue of force, never foreclosing the possibility that war might be needed to enforce the general will of mankind. Wilson had maintained, at least in word, the distinction between truly peace-loving regimes, and others who would have to prove themselves such. The League had failed politically, because the US Senate and the public saw too many contradictions. Later Progressives of both parties, including Hoover, were univocal.

Dropping any kind of test to be applied to regimes, they spoke of "civilized nations" and assumed all were. Later yet, Progressives even dropped "civilized" and assumed fully and directly that all peoples and all governments are created equal and want the same things. War is not the striving of the opposite wills of different peoples or regimes, but rather a kind of disease that afflicts the human species equally, and is subject to one and the same cure. That is why Hoover thought that Kellogg-Briand was an advance over the League:

The European nations have, by the covenant of the League of Nations, agreed that if nations fail to settle their differences peacefully, then force should be applied by other nations to compel them to be reasonable. We have refused to travel this road. We are confident that at least in the Western Hemisphere public opinion will suffice to check violence. This is the road we propose to travel.

Concluded Hoover: "I have no fear that we are not able to impress every country with the single minded good will which lies in the American heart."[4] Hoover and Kellogg knew full well that Aristide Briand and France valued the pact as a backdoor commitment of American support against Germany. But they were comfortable with a commitment that meant different things to different people and that, to them, meant pleasant posturing.

Note well the naturally ill effects of words that mean different things to different people, of pleasing generalities that give false impressions, of what Henry Kissinger would later laud as "creative ambiguity": Among foreigners whose eyes are on the bottom line of international affairs such practices elicit contempt. Among fellow citizens, the attempt to form consensus on a fraudulent basis precludes honest debate and informed choice. An obstacle to understanding the issues, it guarantees disappointment, disillusion, disaffection.

Roosevelt and Hull

President Franklin Roosevelt appointed Cordell Hull as secretary of state in 1933. Hull, who worshiped Woodrow Wilson and served in that post until 1944, longer than anyone before or since, also equated the pursuit of peace with impressing on the world the purity of American intentions. That precluded dealing with concrete challenges to peace. Rather, Roosevelt and Hull urged the rest of the world to follow America's peaceful ways and to build better "mechanisms" for resolving disputes—until events overwhelmed them. In 1937 Hull summed up his and Roosevelt's diplomacy to the world's Chancelleries in a "statement" of the US government's "position in regard to international problems":

This country constantly and consistently advocates maintenance of peace. We advocate national and international self-restraint. We advocate abstinence by all nations from the use of force in pursuit of policy and from interference in the internal affairs of other nations. We advocate adjustment of problems in international relations by processes of peaceful negotiation and agreement. We advocate faithful observance of international agreements . . . modification of provisions of treaties . . . by orderly processes . . . in respect by all nations for the rights of others . . . the revitalizing and strengthening of international law . . . economic security and stability the world over . . . application of the principle of equality of treatment . . . limitation and reduction of armaments . . . cooperative effort by peaceful means in support of the principles hereinbefore stated.[5]

It did not take genius to conclude that Hull and Roosevelt, having used no proper nouns, had no intention of placing any obstacle in the way of any government that was disinclined to follow any or all such generalities, that such inanity was likelier to lead to war than to peace.

Hull's practical fare was to chide Japan for its transgressions against China, to refuse to recognize the permanence of Japanese conquests, and to demand that they be reversed, slowly to deprive Japan of international commerce, never suggesting how the Japanese people might avoid starvation—*while adhering scrupulously to America's treaty commitment not to fortify Guam.* Thus did he threaten and goad, wielding no stick and innocent of strategy. Hoover and Stimson had done less harm by whispering, or shutting up.

President Franklin Roosevelt was even less willing to specify who might trouble America's peace and how, much less what, he thought America might do to preserve it. FDR came into office two years after Japan's invasion of China, and just as Hitler was taking power in Germany. But with regard to neither country did Roosevelt urge a diminution of expectations, nor did he increase America's power. Nor does it take much scrutiny to see that his reputation for awakening America from pacifism is a partisan montage.

Henry Kissinger has characterized Roosevelt's famous "quarantine" speech of 1937 as "brilliantly insincere." Kissinger argues that "Roosevelt was careful not to spell out what he meant" by "quarantine" or anything else, and careful to voice common nostrums. Yet Roosevelt, according to Kissinger, "had a plan" by which to lead the American people to recognize the dire reality facing them. *If that is so, the plan is extrinsic to anything Roosevelt said or did.*

To remove doubt about FDR's *practical* understanding of peace, it is enough to look at what he did not do, and apparently did not consider doing, in the five years between 1936 and America's formal entry into World War II. In 1936, when Hitler placed himself in a position to wage war by sending troops into the Rhineland in violation of the Versailles Treaty, France sought America's *diplomatic* support for pushing the Germans to withdraw their troops. FDR said no. In 1937, when Japan invaded the main part of China and General Douglas MacArthur pleaded once again to fortify Guam and Manila, FDR said no. In 1938–39, after Britain and France had given Czechoslovakia to Hitler, and Hitler was deciding whether to strike eastward or westward, FDR could have kept war out of Western Europe (and kept the United States out of the eventual Stalin–Hitler war) by being the *diplomatic* catalyst and backstop of a (then) daunting Franco-British alliance. Such diplomatic actions might well have produced peace for America. Instead, FDR continued to abstract from reality.

"The political situation in the world," said FDR in 1937, "is growing progressively worse." If it gets much worse, America may not escape harm, no matter how hard she tries. If that is not to happen, "the peace loving nations of the world must make a concerted effort to uphold laws and principles on which alone peace can rest secure." But instead of making any such efforts, Roosevelt added his voice to what had become the Progressive School Solution: speak loudly. "There must be a return to a belief in the pledged word, in the value of a signed treaty. There must be a recognition of the fact that national morality is as vital as private morality." It might take as many as twenty years to make this happen. As many as twenty! But FDR said: "must." It just *had* to happen. "If civilization is to survive, the principles of the Prince of Peace must be restored. Shattered trust between nations must be revived."[6]

How to make these things happen, Roosevelt did not hint. Rather, he deepened the American people's innocence of the bloody methods by which the real *Princeps Pacis* had established the Augustan age's peace. Roosevelt did not name any source of international troubles. He called them "an epidemic," "a contagion"—things conveniently impersonal and politically neutral, because he wanted to give the impression that they were outside the realm of responsibility of nations and individuals, especially himself.

Dr. Roosevelt prescribed the standard remedy for plagues: quarantine. In the context of international affairs the term means nothing, except steering clear of the infected areas, and it corresponded to no actions taken by the US government.

Roosevelt's September 3, 1939, speech—*after* the Munich Pact, *after* the violation thereof, *after* the Stalin-Hitler Pact, *after* the invasion of Poland, two days *after* the outbreak of World War II—was not measurably different. The villain was impersonal: force itself, regardless of who used it or why. Nobody was at fault. No nation threatened America any more than any other. America must act not for discrete objectives and interests, but solely to achieve Utopia. "[T]he unfortunate events of these recent years have been based on the use of force or the threat of force. And it seems to me that . . . the influence of America should be consistent in seeking for humanity a final peace which will eliminate as far as it is possible to do so, the continued use of force among nations."[7] As Wilson had said, the only peace worthy of America would have to be final, once and forever more. But, please, no details.

Only on December 29, 1940—a half-year *after* the fall of France, *after* Dunkirk, by which time Hitler had won the war (no one could know that he would throw it all away by invading Russia in 1941)—did Roosevelt indict "the Nazi masters of Germany." There followed words that his cousin Theodore might have written a generation before:

Does anyone seriously believe that we need fear attack while a free Britain remains our most powerful naval neighbor in the Atlantic? Does anyone seriously believe, on the other hand, that we could rest easy if the Axis powers were our neighbor there?

> If Great Britain goes down, the Axis powers will control the conti-
> nents of Europe, Asia, Africa, Australasia, and the high seas. . . . It
> is no exaggeration that all of us in the Americas would be living at
> the point of a gun. . . . There is far less chance of the United States
> getting into war if we do all we can now to support the nations
> defending themselves against attack by the Axis than if we acqui-
> esce in their defeat.[8]

But by then Germany had given up preparations for invading Britain, because Britain had already won the Battle of Britain. So what,
exactly, did FDR want to accomplish by this gesture?

History does not record an answer, in part because Franklin
Roosevelt did not allow the American public to consider the question. It is by no means clear whether he had done so himself. By
March 1941, Roosevelt had agreed to supply armaments to Britain.
By September he had ordered the US Navy convoying them to "shoot
on sight" any German vessels they saw on the way. This meant waging war, of course. But a state of war did not exist and Roosevelt was
adamant that it should not. Nor did he say anything specific about
the peace he desired or about how he intended to achieve it.

Did Roosevelt's ends and means match America's interests? To
answer such questions, anti-interventionists asked Roosevelt to
submit to Congress a formal declaration of war against Germany.
Roosevelt refused and suggested that those who insisted on a clear
choice between peace and war were isolationists, fascists, and anti-
Semites.

Understanding Franklin Roosevelt's tergiversations on war and
peace requires keeping in mind that the Soviet Union and Nazi
Germany were allied between August 1939 and June 1941; that this
was the alliance that had started the war; that Roosevelt was riding
the consensus of the Democratic Party, and that in the 1930s and
40s this party contained Communists devoted to the Soviet Union's
success; hence that keeping the Democratic Party together required
being steadfastly pro-Soviet.

Since another part of FDR's Progressive constituency was pro-
Nazi, especially between 1949 and 1941 that meant straddling
the totalitarian powers, their victims, and America's interests. In

November 1940, the Nazi sympathies of Joseph P. Kennedy, one of FDR's important constituents, led to his resignation as ambassador to Britain. That straddle began the unraveling of the Democratic coalition that eventually led to the party's losses beginning in 1946. Moreover, in deference to the white ethnic elements of the Democratic Party, Roosevelt could not go too far in his praise of the Soviet Union beyond such generalities as calling it a defender of "freedom of conscience, freedom of religion"—already a perilous stretch.

So, the most expedient way to handle intra-Democratic difficulties was to insult Republicans. But this worsened war abroad and strife at home.

Looming danger had opened but a small breach in the intellectual wall that pacifism had erected against common sense. Neither FDR nor America's progressive ruling class asked the fundamental question: what must we do to secure our peace vis-à-vis the Germans and Japanese? If we use American military power, what conditions do we want to establish that will satisfy our needs and those of the troublesome nations? In other words, what are our concrete diplomatic objectives—objectives that would become the aims of our military operations? How much power might we need to force such a peace?

Perhaps if we had stated those objectives to friend and foe alike, plus our determination to force them, we would not have had to fight. Certainly, if America were quickly to have fortified Guam and Manila Bay, Japan could not have made war in the Pacific. If the Rooseveltians had looked at the Soviet Union as something other than a paradigm of their ideology, they would have been able to gauge its existential threat to America's peace.

In sum, though Franklin Roosevelt had become open to the use of force, and then well-nigh addicted to it, he never shed Progressive pacifism or raw domestic partisanship enough to regard war and diplomacy as tools for crafting arrangements to resolve current problems, arrangements in which all could live in peace until unforeseen ones arose.

And the war came.

16

War for Everything, and Nothing

A concrete concept of peace is the only compass through the fog of war. The statesman must steer by that compass no less than the helmsman by magnets (today, GPS). By the time Pearl Harbor plunged America into war, forty years of Progressive pacifism had imbued America's ruling class with conviction that war is a relic of a bygone age, that, if there is to be peace at all, it must be a kind of Utopia. The Progressive catechism taught that establishing peace in perpetuity requires merely removing the retrograde, criminal elements that stand in its way, that thinking in terms of national interest and spheres of influence is evidence of warmongering. Statesmen did not have to reason about details, nor expose their reasoning to the people's judgment. Woodrow Wilson had replaced the compass of concrete peace with a utopian creed. Blinkered by this creed, backed by blind power, Roosevelt led America through World War II. But by thus foreordaining the lack of peace that followed, Roosevelt furthered the erosion of America's body politic that Wilson had begun.

Hostile as the Progressive creed was to calculating the peace that is to follow war, it proved all too compatible with blind hatred of the enemy. On December 7, 1941, the American people wanted vengeance against Japan. Four days later, Germany placed itself in the line of hate by declaring war against the United States. But what did America's leaders mean to accomplish by wrecking these countries, beyond the indispensable objective of defeating their armed forces? Franklin Roosevelt and his class answered with utopian nonsense. This on December 9: "Not only must the shame of Japan's treachery be wiped out, but the sources of international brutality, wherever they exist, be wiped out."[1] And on January 6, 1942: "[W]e are fighting to cleanse the world of ancient evils, ancient ills."[2] What these were, he never bothered to explain, never mind what the cleansing agent might be.

Damn the Details

FDR's demand for "unconditional surrender," meaning content-free cessation of hostilities in the name of uncompromising-but-undefined morality, confirmed that his class could not agree on war aims—that Roosevelt's class was intellectually bankrupt. In practice, keeping the German and Japanese people guessing what America had in mind for them lengthened the war—as did the militarily senseless burning and blasting of millions of civilians. But it legitimized unconditional aid to Stalin, and *allowed America's leaders not to soil their hands with the messy details of peacemaking until events had largely tied those hands.*

Any war, any peace, is about details. Charles de Gaulle, like everyone else who tried to engage Roosevelt in discussions of the war's concrete issues—how belligerents would relate to one another, to Germany, Japan, Poland, East Asia, etc.—noted that Roosevelt painted seductive pictures with broad strokes.[3] Like Wilson, FDR paid little mind to concrete matters, because, as far as one can tell from what he said and did, his eye seemed fixed on the abstract picture of world progress, whose agent he imagined himself. Moral commitment to that, more than any cynicism, explains his willingness to make Faustian bargains with Stalin—the only power with whose help he hoped to change the world, to escape power politics forever, to end humanity's endless struggling—a power not incidentally favored by a substantial wing of his party. That moral commitment on the highest level of generalization, buttressed by domestic politics, overrode more specific, more concrete thoughts about the American people's interests.

The August 14, 1941, Anglo-American "Atlantic Charter" that the US government trumpeted to the planet promised "no territorial changes that did not accord with the freely expressed wishes of the people concerned . . . the right of all peoples to choose the

form of government under which they will live." But the Atlantic
Charter also abstracted from the question that American statesmen
are obliged to address as fiduciary representatives of the American
people: What are the people's concrete interests in this war? What
is to be our peace? What, specifically, must we do to earn it? Under
the guise of postponing planning for the outcome of hostilities until
hostilities had ceased, FDR let the general override the specific. It
was easier that way, intellectually and politically. Commonsense says
that operations of war serve to secure the characteristics of peace.
FDR's reversal of commonsense resulted in Cold War.

Stalin's Mortgage

The cost of achieving military victory over enemies-in-arms necessarily mortgages the peace. Because the size and terms of such mortgages naturally reduce the worth of any peace, negotiating them
and keeping close tabs on adherence to the fine print can make all
the difference between outcomes that are worth the cost and ones
that are not. The main problem with American statecraft in World
War II is that cooperation with the Soviet Union was part of the
war's cost, and that it was obvious at the outset to anyone who cared
to look that this cost must diminish to some extent the quality of
the peace. But to what extent? Hence the necessity to calibrate and
recalibrate precise arrangements to minimize that cost should have
been obvious.

History contradicts the historians' standard excuse, that the
Rooseveltians did not really know that Stalin meant to trash the
Atlantic Charter. But Polish and Ukrainian Americans, as well as
the Catholic Church, warned of that unceasingly, which is one reason why the Rooseveltians supported the Atlantic Charter publicly
until late 1944 (having abandoned it privately as soon as they proclaimed it); Winston Churchill, certain that Stalin meant to take as
much of Eastern Europe as he could, urged Roosevelt from January
1942 through the Yalta Conference three years later to negotiate
a specific, enforceable delineation of spheres of influence with the
USSR. But FDR and his class looked away, because they would
neither soil perpetual peace with spheres of influence nor risk

displeasing the disparate political constituencies that sustained their administration.

While America was still at peace, the practical, proximate objective might have been to stay at peace, to build strength while channeling as much of the war as possible to the Nazi-Soviet front. Even as World War II broke out, it was clear that reversing its ill effects would eventually require depriving Stalin, as well as Hitler, of as much as possible of what they had gained from their Pact of August 1939—the war's first and most consequential act of violence.

Yet, when Hitler invaded Russia in 1941, it became just as obvious that aiding Stalin was the sine qua non of defeating Hitler. Hence depriving Stalin of his gains would have to mean, at the very least, calibrating aid to him quantitatively, qualitatively, and chronologically. Roosevelt refused to listen to proposals for doing that, and kept people in charge of the aid program who did the same.

Just as surely, depriving Hitler of his gains required aid to Britain. But American aid rendered to Britain tended to divert Hitler's resources to the Western front, whereas it was US interest to push the war as much as possible to the Eastern front in order to facilitate the totalitarians' mutual exhaustion. Stalin wanted America to join a Western "second front" as soon as possible. But America's interest required joining the Western front as late as possible, when a Germany exhausted by death-struggle in the East would be eager to surrender to the West. Instead of weighing these considerations, the Rooseveltians committed to helping Stalin and joining the Western front quickly, massively, and with little forethought.

The onset of war should have underlined the urgency of any number of specific questions about what peace America should seek. How far into Europe should we suffer Soviet influence to spread before we began treating Stalin as an enemy? For what was it worthwhile to spend American lives, and for what not? What kind of postwar Germany would suit our peace? Even in 1944, when that question could no longer be avoided, Franklin Roosevelt signed off on the Morgenthau Plan that would have converted Germany into a country of "primarily agricultural and pastoral character." But Secretary of War Henry L Stimson wrote that, when confronted, FDR "was frankly staggered by this and said he had no idea how he could have initialed this, that he had evidently done it without much thought."[4]

The time for minimizing Stalin's mortgage on the postwar world was when he most needed the West's help and had least power to assert his will over Europe—that is, in 1942. The earlier the negotiations, the likelier they would have been to produce terms closer to the Western position. In December 1941, Stalin actually proposed to Churchill a postwar arrangement that excluded some of the gains the USSR had made in the Stalin-Hitler Pact. He was willing to bargain because he had to. But, early and late, the Rooseveltians' totally public but totally toothless and insincere support of the Atlantic Charter, as well as their refusal to define spheres of influence, gave Stalin only two choices: give up any and all gains from the Soviet Union's epic sacrifices, including the dominion over the Baltic States and Eastern Poland, or wait until he was able to disdain what, by May 1945, were mere pleas from the West. Roosevelt made Stalin's decision easy.

Would any attempt to limit Stalin's capacity to trouble the postwar peace have decreased his cooperation in the war? To the West, Stalin's cooperation was important until mid-1943. But to Stalin, American food, trucks, and countless other items were vital until the war's very last days. Moreover, while the West was always in a position to make some accommodation with Germany (not Hitler) even just tacitly, Stalin never was. Thus, in 1944, George F. Kennan advised Roosevelt to lay America's winning cards on the table and play them for their full worth.[5] But the Rooseveltians never considered doing that.

Instead, the Rooseveltians debased America's cause by identifying it with Stalin's. The 1946 trials of Nazi leaders at Nuremberg were prototypical. Justice Robert Jackson of the US Supreme Court presided over the conviction of Hitler's foreign minister Joachim von Ribbentrop for signing the Hitler-Stalin pact of 1939, while the other signer, Stalin's foreign minister Vyacheslav Molotov sat with the accusers. There and thereafter, the Rooseveltians and their Progressive successors treated the Soviet Union's full partnership in unleashing World War II as a non-event. By using the totalitarian tactic of intellectual air-brushing to try justifying their Soviet affections, they poisoned American political life.

In Asia, where our commitment to China had outrun our power between 1900 and 1945, would we now maintain or extend the hegemony gained by war, or reduce that commitment, or both? Instead of choosing between alternatives, our statesmen embraced a contradiction: They pretended that the Soviet Union adhered to the war aims set forth in the Atlantic Charter, but refused to define whether the peace that Americans and Britons were dying for would secure the freedom of China. Rather, they hazarded and lost China's freedom by making concessions to the Soviet Union in Europe to hasten its totally unnecessary (and counterproductive) entry into the war against Japan.

We will never know how ready the American people were for specific discussion of peace objectives. We do know that America's ruling class never was ready, because it was crippled by pacifist ideology as well as by incompatible commitments to freedom and to Stalin.

Franklin Roosevelt may have imagined that sidestepping specificity left his options open. Instead, it created blank spaces that others around him filled—not least Harry Hopkins, who acted as "deputy president" throughout the war and whom the Soviet KGB considered its agent of influence, and Alger Hiss, an agent of Soviet military intelligence, the GRU.

From Chungking to Algiers, US officials had to play it by ear, Washington not having given them a compass by which to steer their decisions about which local factions to support or oppose with America's growing power. Alas, they developed a taste for tinkering.

The UN Dodge

The Rooseveltians dodged questions about postwar peace by erecting and worshiping the United Nations Organizations, a totem to whose allegedly omnipotent and omnibenevolent power they abdicated the future. It is difficult to exaggerate the hopes that America's foreign policy establishment poured into what they assumed would be an instrument of US-Soviet co-dominion, the efforts they made to inculcate them into the American people, or the credulity they demanded and briefly got.

The blindness of their fervor may be seen in Harry Hopkins's reflection on the Yalta Conference of 1945:

> In our hearts we really believed a new day had dawned, the day we had for so many years longed for and about which we had talked so much. We were all convinced we had won the first great victory for peace, and when I say we, I mean all of us, all civilized mankind. The Russians had proved that they could be reasonable and far-sighted and neither the President nor any one of us had the slightest doubt that we could live with them and get on peaceably with them far into the future. I must, however, make one reservation—I believe that in our hearts we made the proviso that we couldn't foretell how things would turn out if something happened to Stalin.[6]

The catalogue of the American foreign policy establishment's sacrifices to Stalin for the sake of the UN, from the sacrifice of Poland to the rendition of prisoners of war to Stalin's Gulag, is beyond our scope. Suffice it to say that ritual obeisance to the UN remained de rigueur among America's "best and brightest" years after FDR himself had conceded privately that he had misjudged the Soviets. Thus, for example, Senator Arthur Vandenberg's February 1946 speech to the Senate touting the theme that peace depended on the UN: ". . . the world's only hope of organized peace and security is inevitably linked with the evolution and destiny of this United Nations Organization."[7]

Having first cut the people out of deliberations on their peace, the Rooseveltians then corrupted the people's capacity to engage in them by promoting the nonsense that all the UN's members are equal, equally united in the love of peace, and eager to take others' opinions into consideration in "the parliament of man." Schools and communities across America were encouraged to organize local "Model UN" conferences, in which individuals took on the roles of member nations. Adults as well as children even played the roles of

Byelorussia and Ukraine, to whose independence and equality among nations the UN charter attested but which all knew were merely two extra votes that the United States had granted to Stalin. In these conclaves, Americans playing what they presumed to be the roles of foreign powers solved the world's problems in a few hours and wondered innocently why their diplomats could not do the same. The National Council of Churches and the United Nations Association of the United States of America infused into America's religious and civic capillaries the message that the choice was between peace through the UN or Armageddon.

It took a generation for this to become a laughing stock.

Though, by 1947, the US foreign policy establishment ceased to expect any significant good from the UN, it never ceased paying obeisance to it, and not just because doing so would indict its earlier judgment. In the early years, continuing to pretend that the UN matters let American statesmen pretend to abdicate responsibility for having failed to achieve real peace. By 1950, American statesmen had learned that conducting the policies they chose with the endorsement by the UN, beginning with the Korean War, allowed them to *parry questions at home about whether they were acting wisely by asserting that they were acting legitimately.*

In our time, pretend-obeisance to the UN became a means by which the Bush administrations, followed by the Clinton and Obama administrations, have asserted the right to make war and peace as they please regardless of the US body politic. This masks thinly an assertion of authority over war and peace reminiscent of absolute monarchy.

Self-Deception by Generality

The war further confirmed our statesmen's habit of transmuting pertinent questions into meaningless generalities, rooted in the Progressive era's substitution of what amounts to the ruling class's code for the active verbs and proper nouns of dictionaries and grammar books. The Progressives had stressed that popular control of foreign policy would guarantee peace. Wilson had proclaimed from the housetops that henceforth foreign policy would be made in the light of day. But Wilson, Roosevelt, and their successors used every means available to shield their reasoning about war and peace from the American people. Refraining from specificity, they argue, leaves them with more options—freer. Alas, not having to explain to fellow citizens what they intend frees them from explaining it fully to themselves as well—dumber.

The most immediate result was that the Second World War in Europe, fought nominally by nations united in pursuit of abstract peace and universal freedom, resulted in two spheres of influence divided by an Iron Curtain with more people under governments more despotic than ever before, waging "cold war" against one another, and ready for mutual annihilation. Because the US government's explanation for why things had turned out so came from divided counsels, they fostered domestic antagonism. Was treason by Communist agents and spies in the US government's upper echelons responsible? Or had excessive care for Poland and insufficient solicitude toward Russia turned a good ally into an enemy?

The best defense for the outcome was "it could have been worse." A truism, but irrelevant. The practical truth is that the statesmen responsible for securing peace, their minds filled with other priorities, had forgotten statesmanship's paramount priority. Worse, the Cold War would teach them that managing endless conflict could be an end in itself, and a profitable career.

17

Cold War

The Cold War pushed the idea of peace further into the recesses of the American ruling class's collective mind. During the Cold War a "national-security establishment" grew, including Republicans and Democrats, government officials, and their "bench" in universities and the media—many thousands who make a good living from National Security—a class who became ever less diverse in outlook over the last half of the twentieth century. This establishment is precisely what Alexander Hamilton and James Madison had feared in *Federalist* #25 and #41. As this part of the ruling class's outlook on war and peace became more specialized, it diverged further from the commonsense of the American people. During the Cold War, it made choices about war and peace in intellectual terms increasingly incomprehensible to the American body politic and corrosive of it.

Eternal and Novel

During the Cold War, neither the United States nor the USSR contended for a concrete vision of peace. According to Soviet theory, the victory of socialism would establish peace forever as it ended history by resolving all human contradictions. But the USSR's practical objective was empire over Eastern Europe and destabilization everywhere else—that is, endless strife. America's national-security establishment for its part came to believe that, because the Soviet Union was eternal, so would the "twilight struggle" be, and hence that the Cold War itself was also eternal and was such peace as the world would ever know. By such parallel agreement that peace belonged to the past, American leaders helped to change America's mentality in ways they no one imagined.

Still, the two sides represented contrasting notions of how life should be lived. Which would succeed in affirming and which would have to negate what it was all about? George F. Kennan's *Foreign Affairs* article of 1947, "The Sources of Soviet Conduct," had forecast that "containment" of Soviet ambitions would lead to the regime's transformation and restore international normalcy. America needed only to reaffirm what it is about and keep strong. This version of containment meant defeating the USSR's attempts to expand its empire, while successful revolts within its empire disheartened it. This was consistent with J. Q. Adams's 1823 response to Russia's monarchical pretensions in the New World. But though some of the American ruling class's rhetoric and practices during the Cold War's early years were profoundly conservative, its collective mind contained ideas that eventually banished peace from it. They prevailed eventually, because the Cold War grew its own dynamic, the essence of which was the pretense of its own radical novelty.

American Cold War thought built upon a half-century of intellectual attempts to avoid the hard details of peace and war through thaumaturgic generalities. The following is an account of the ideas that denatured and stripped the concept of peace from our collective mind during the Cold War and weakened allegiance to America's historic uniqueness. We confine ourselves here to the logic of ideas, and defer until the next chapter consideration of how the not-so-small wars of the period contributed to this outcome.

Containment's Unraveling Compromise

The American body politic in general and the Democratic Party in particular had adopted the concept of containment as a compromise between pursuing peace by accepting the Communist world's expansion or by rolling it back. As that compromise unraveled over nearly a half-century, Americans waged a hot political war among themselves, the consequences of which are with us yet. In fact, "containment" merely papered over the deepening chasm between Americans who had accepted at face value the Progressive proposition that peace means espousal of the historical inevitability of Progressive forces (including the Soviet Union), and those who believed that the United States has both right and duty to preserve its uniqueness by force.

The dialectic between the two visions was driven by the notion, increasingly predominant in the Democratic Party, that some kind of "negotiation" or "deal" was the only alternative to general war. *The question: "deal or war" came to overshadow "what is to be America's peace?" and,* a fortiori, questions about *the quality of any "deal."* The Republican Party followed close behind.

This is how it happened. In 1953 and 1956, East Germans and Hungarians, respectively, revolted against Soviet rule and wrested control of their capital cities. They asked for American help. The Soviets, reeling from Stalin's death, did nothing. Original "containment" had anticipated and looked forward to such opportunities. But Republican Secretary of State John Foster Dulles convinced the president to refuse help, thus abandoning the *offensive* half of "containment." The Soviets reasserted control.

Then, in 1961, The Democratic administration that followed the US elections of 1960 qualified America's theretofore categorical promise to respond to any Soviet attack on Europe with a nuclear attack on the Soviet Union. It also manifested unwillingness to insist on Western rights of access to all Berlin and acceptance of the infamous Berlin Wall. By so doing, it gave up its commitment to uphold the provisional peace of 1945 and undermined containment's *defensive* half.

This engendered a sense that the Soviet Union had the wind in its sails, and led to a sea change in Western European politics: Whereas, prior to 1961, Europeans led by Germany's Konrad Adenauer and France's Charles de Gaulle had pressed Americans for the most steadfast version of "containment," thereafter Europeans became the foremost advocates of peace by some kind of "deal"—meaning accommodation. For example, Germany's Social Democratic Party, which had been the most anti-Soviet of its kind in Europe, reversed its 1959 *Bad Godesberg* platform and became the most accommodating. This "Atlantic crisis," as Robert Kleiman described it in his 1964 book, *Atlantic Crisis: American Diplomacy Confronts a*

Resurgent Europe, lent support to those in America who favored that very course. This cycle gathered force to the point that, beginning in the late 1960s, not displeasing accommodation-minded Europeans became the principal argument for ratcheting US-Soviet relations to favor giving the Soviet Union an ever-freer hand in Europe.

Thus did the American ruling class follow the course of events it had set in motion.

By the 1970s Henry Kissinger (through Republican President Gerald Ford and Ambassador Helmut Sonnenfeldt) had thus framed the American ruling class's bipartisan consensus on US-Soviet relations: The United States should work hard and hazard much to bring the Soviet Union into the community of nations, while facilitating its hold on its empire. By that logic, Americans who opposed that consensus were enemies of peace. That had become George Kennan's view, as well. By this logic, these Americans' view of the Cold War— "we win, they lose" (as Ronald Reagan encapsulated it)—was illegitimate. By extension, so was their view of America itself. Hence it was understandable that, as shown by the Mitrokhin Archive and post-Soviet revelations in the Moscow newspaper *Izvestia,* Senator Edward Kennedy (D-MA) offered to cooperate with Soviet leaders to defeat such Americans in the name of peace and progress.[1]

So strong was this bipartisan ruling-class consensus that, as the Soviet Union was collapsing in 1989–91, the Republican George H. W. Bush administration extended untied loans to the Soviet Union, urged restive nationalities within it to refrain from seceding (*vide* George H. W. Bush's speech in Kiev, July 31, 1991, drafted by Condoleezza Rice, later George W. Bush's secretary of state), and proposed saving East Germany as part of a federation with the West, even as East Germans were walking away from it.

In short, the ruling class had turned George Kennan's vision of peace through "containment" inside out, and was groping toward some hybrid of the Soviet vision. But when the Soviet Union died on Christmas day 1991, its vision of peace and practice of strife became historical curiosities. By then, though, the American ruling class had shed the capacity to think about peace and normalcy. As we will see in Chapter 19, it had become addicted to the practice of something like empire.

Pseudo-technical Fog

Refusal to think seriously about nuclear weapons also exacerbated aversion to rational thought about war and peace and contributed to pacifism more amoral than that of the Interwar Years. Does nuclear energy's capacity easily to destroy cities overturn ordinary reasoning about war and peace? Does it mandate that America abandon its conception of itself? The American ruling class did not deny that genocide by fire and sword had been routine in the ancient world, or that governments in our time have killed tens of millions through starvation and extermination camps, or that the effects of nuclear weapons, like those of all others, depend on those who use them and on those against whom they are used. They simply labeled it immoral to counter the dogma that the atomic bomb is "the ultimate weapon," and affirmed that the alternative forevermore can be only between total peace and the annihilation of mankind.

Three score and ten years during which we have had neither peace nor annihilation have not shaken that dogma's hold. Facts seem powerless against it.

"Safety will be the sturdy child of terror, and survival the twin brother of annihilation." Thus did Winston Churchill sum up the conventional wisdom that took hold of Euro-American elites after the Hiroshima bomb. Bernard Brodie's book, *The Absolute Weapon: Atomic Power and World Order,* written in October 1945, asserted that, forevermore, both the United States and Soviet Union could utterly destroy each other and neither could protect itself. This, near a half-decade before the Soviet Union had "the bomb" and a decade and a half before the first intercontinental missiles, more than a generation before anything like a balance between US and Soviet forces. Movies like "On the Beach" (1959) touted as true the absurdity that mankind itself would perish after a nuclear war. Harvard songster Tom Lehrer summed up the all-or-nothing mindlessness of the 1950s–1970s: "We will all go together when we go"—so popular because it relieved so many of intellectual and moral responsibilities. No surprise then, when Herman Kahn published *On Thermonuclear War* (1959), detailing the enormous differences that strategy and tactics would make in the peace that would follow a

nuclear war, the American ruling class devised intellectual stratagems to evade the book's insertion of reason into the elite's *schaden-
freude* about nukes.

In the late 1950s, data from the U-2 spy plane having made it
possible to choose how to fight the Soviet Union in ways that would
minimize damage to the United States, US military planers set about
building forces to do just that. But, by 1963, US Defense Secretary
Robert McNamara had concluded that keeping such forces adequate
to this task through continued modernization was more expensive
than building *a set of forces that would guarantee peace forever.*
Such forces would perform this wonder by preparing to kill 25 percent of the Soviet population and to destroy 50 percent of its industry, while doing nothing to hinder the Soviets from doing the same to
America. This would be forever because mankind had climbed onto
an eternal "technological plateau."

This became ruling class ideology. Accordingly, because vulner-
ability fosters peace, while defense is provocative of war, US anti-
aircraft defenses were dismantled and US antimissile defenses have
not been built to this day. That the Soviet Union did not share this
view and built its forces to fight, survive, and win did not dent this
fantasy. Remarkably, neither did the Soviet Union's disappearance.

Consistent with this logic, beginning in the 1960s and into our
time, our ruling class reprised the vision of peace of such as Charles
Evans Hughes, William Borah, and Cordell Hull: since armaments
cause (or contribute to) international antagonisms, treaties to control or reduce them lead to peace. Thus Henry Kissinger told the US
Senate that his 1972 antimissile defense treaty had secured the new
and everlasting age's promise of peace.

In our time, as in the Interwar Years, it is still dogma that the
United States can lead the way by adhering to such treaties even
when the other side violates them. The Reagan administration was
not immune to this. Its 1987 Top Secret National Security Decision
Directive 192 acknowledged that the Soviet Union had violated the
1972 treaty, but stated that the US would answer violation with
"exemplary compliance." In 2012, President Barack Obama com-
municated to Russia confidentially that, after his expected reelection,
he would forswear missile defenses more thoroughly than before,

previous commitments notwithstanding. Vastly different public rhetoric has masked remarkable consistency.

Whereas, during the Interwar period, the attitudes of America's ruling class on peace and war had reflected to some extent the American
people's sentiments, during the Cold War they ran against the grain
of popular bellicosity toward America's Communist enemies. This
happened because, by the mid-twentieth century, our ruling class
had become convinced of its intellectual and moral superiority over
the American people. Conscious, however, that departing from popular opinion is democratically dangerous, the Cold War ruling class
spoke increasingly in pseudo-technical terms that amounted to a private language impenetrable to the uninitiated.

Beginning in the 1960s, official documents spoke of "assured
destruction" to be achieved by spreading "megaton equivalents" to
reach the "flat of the curve of the 20psi circle." To achieve such "suf-
ficiency," in "counter-value targeting," the "throw weight" of missiles
was irrelevant. By contrast, "counterforce targeting" was "destabi-
lizing" while defenses against missiles and bombers were not "cost
effective." The Soviets had invested in both, but only because they had
not yet absorbed the Americans' new wisdom. Therefore, although
this approach of theirs would produce "asymmetrical" damages to
very different things, and hence "mutual assured destruction" would
not be really so "mutual," there was no reason to worry because
"minimum deterrence" would ensure "overall balance." English
translation: cut American strategic forces. Whatever else this foggy
lingo did, it relieved those who used it of the need to justify their
doings, their salaries and their status, likely even to themselves.

Arcane language enhanced the notion that, in the age of nuclear
weapons and high technology, the business of war and peace had
become so complicated as to transcend dictionaries. That, and the
secrecy that necessarily surrounds nuclear weapons and espionage,
helped a new class of pseudo-academic "experts" to convince ordinary citizens that matters of war and peace are beyond their understanding, and to shoehorn them into acceptance of a less peaceful
peace and a much less autonomous America.

Thomas Schelling's book *The Strategy of Conflict* (1960)—Schelling
won the 2005 Nobel Prize for economics—was one of the intellectual

fountainheads of America's conduct of the Cold War's long latter period. Colleges sentenced countless students to think in the book's lingo, which assumes that international affairs are contests between interchangeable units, each seeking to maximize gains and minimize losses within an inescapable matrix of choices. The point of the ensuing "game theory" was to show the irrationality of the United States pursuing other than an accommodation with the Soviet Union (or for that matter anyone else), given that the others could not do otherwise. Since the matrix is defined as inescapable, it defined pursuit of one's own peace as illusory. Henry Kissinger's *Nuclear Weapons and Foreign Policy* (1957) and *The Necessity for Choice: Prospects of American Foreign Policy* (1960) translated Schelling's lingo into English and promoted a class of white-coated conflict managers (Kissinger, and Kissinger wannabes) who claimed to know how to adjust competing claims according to the Realist-rational matrix.

These conflict managers counseled, and helped to lead America in a host of commitments, the limits of which they imagined were set by such matrices. The Vietnam War was the foremost of these. It did not turn out according to the conflict managers' ideology.

The National-Security Establishment

In sum, arguably the Cold War's biggest legacy was the class (many thousands in our time) who imagined themselves, and who had managed to be regarded as, entitled by expertise to conduct America's business of war and peace—indeed, the whole world's business of war and peace—but who had nothing but contempt for the American people's desire for their own peace, and for the notion that such peace is realizable. Grown during the Cold War, this class mentality and personal interest in managing perpetual conflict survived the Cold War's passing. This national-security class lives to conduct, and lives by conducting, perpetual twilight struggle. For it, peace is inconvenient personally as well as intellectually.

18

No-Win War, No Peace

From George Washington through Theodore Roosevelt, American statesmen stored up with the American people a reservoir of trust on matters of war and peace. Their successors have drawn on it following a pattern: They decide to "do something [military]" about some events somewhere because "doing nothing" would be dangerous. But then, because they deem defeating the enemy (perhaps, even, identifying the enemy) to be even more dangerous than "doing nothing," they decide to send Americans to kill and die without a plan for peace. The default compromise between "doing it" to establish peace or not at all turns out to be, as Chairman of the Joint Chiefs of Staff General Omar Bradley said about Korea, to "fight it out in general" on the basis of trust in the ruling class's sophistication. In the course of succeeding generations, that sophistication reduced the American people's elected representatives' participation in foreign affairs, produced less peace with foreign nations, shrank America's reservoir of trust, and undermined the American regime's domestic legitimacy.

Korea

In 1949 Secretary of State Dean Acheson, with the advice and consent of chief foreign policy planner, George F. Kennan, had publicly placed South Korea outside the US defense perimeter—presumably because they judged it irrelevant to America's peace. In 1950, after North Korea's Soviet-inspired-and-supplied invasion, Acheson, Kennan, President Truman, and the rest of the US ruling class hurried to send America's armed forces to the Korean Peninsula.

Had they made a mistake to which they now owned up, or were they reacting to embarrassment and panic? Did they now truly judge that Korea was essential to America's peace, because the USSR was breaking out of containment, and, hence, that communism must be defeated there? Was our peace now at stake? If so, why not subdue the enemy—why not win—in a way that would secure that peace? But if, as General Bradley told Congress, Korea was "The wrong war, at the wrong place, at the wrong time, and with the wrong enemy,"[1] why kill and die in it?

Our ruling class did not answer such questions so much as it suggested that Americans who asked them showed lack of sophistication. Trying to impose our peace on the enemy, said President Truman, would make for "wider war," which had to mean nuclear annihilation. Americans doubted that, and insisted: win or get out. No matter: they were too unsophisticated to understand. Because questions of war and peace are beyond the American people's understanding, their insistence in meddling in their betters' prerogatives is illegitimate.

While the latter-day American ruling class's claims that war and peace are its exclusive bailiwick is on bases different from those of Baroque kings, the claim's effect is not so different. The commonplace that the Cold War shifted power over peace and war from the legislative to the executive branch overshadows the underlying fact that the power went not so much from one set of the American people's representatives to another, but that it went from elected officials responsible to the voters to professionals who are not—persons whose personal interest in the management of international affairs is more pressing than whatever impersonal interest they may have in the people's peace.

The dichotomy between the people and the professionals grew when the end of the military draft practically exempted the classes who decide about war from the direct consequences thereof. Hence during the twentieth century's second half and into the twenty-first, America's ruling class has used various stratagems to minimize Congress's involvement in decisions about war and peace as well as to limit popular discussion of them, arguing that the American people's judgment is not to be trusted. That this has resulted in less peace and more war surprises no one familiar with history.

After the 1950 invasion of Korea, such peace as "containment" promised depended on teaching the Communist powers to regret that invasion and not to try anything like it again. Alas, our ruling class's Korea policy, by swallowing casualties in the name of self-restraint, taught the Communist powers the opposite: that our ruling class had given up seeking America's peace and hence that it was safe to look for more opportunities to bleed Americans.

Vietnam

That became clear after 1954, when the USSR and China sponsored North Vietnam's invasion of South Vietnam. Our ruling class, wary of Korea-scale casualties but still unwilling to choose between fighting for its own version of peace (about which they argued among themselves) or letting the enemy have his, at first engaged just a few military advisers who were supposed to "nation-build" South Vietnam so that it could fight on its own. When the Communist powers did not give America peace on the cheap, our ruling class, informed by America's most highly credentialed academics, committed US forces slowly, hoping that the enemy would be daunted by the prospect of facing massive American power.

But the Communists had learned the simple lesson—ever so valid today—that *the amount of US power does not matter, so long as the Americans remain wedded to their peculiar idea of sophistication.* More simply: If you don't know what you are doing, your level of effort is irrelevant.

Lyndon Johnson repeated: "there is no victory in Vietnam, for anybody" and defined the enemy there as John F. Kenney had: "poverty, ignorance and disease." But the less sophisticated North Vietnamese followed the straightforward logic of war until, in 1975, one of its tank commanders crashed through the US Embassy's gate in Saigon as Vietnamese who had given their hearts and minds to America had their fingers smashed by US troops as they clung to the skids of the last helicopter fleeing the US rout.

President Johnson spoke that way on the advice of sophisticates like Henry Kissinger, famous for his 1974 dictum: "What in
the name of God is strategic superiority? . . . What do you do with
it?"[2] Our ruling class did not want to think about what anybody's
superiority or victory might mean—what different versions of peace
might mean and was literally frightened that the American people thought about such things. Johnson had won election in 1964
by branding his opponent, Barry Goldwater, as an unsophisticated
warmonger for having said that Americans should choose between
doing whatever it might take to win the Vietnam War or not fighting it. His secretary of defense, Robert McNamara, revealed in his
book *In Retrospect: The Tragedy and Lessons of Vietnam* (1995)
that he considered Goldwater's arguments a greater threat to peace
than anything that the Communist powers might do. By the same
token, Secretary of State Dean Rusk, asked at a 1965 press conference about the possibility that North Vietnam might put captured
Americans on trial, answered that he feared this would incite the
American people to demand victory in Vietnam. "That is not our
policy," said Rusk. Indeed, it was not.

Progressive Consistency

During the Interwar Years, Republicans like William Borah and
Herbert Hoover, and Democrats like Cordell Hull and FDR, had
profited politically by accusing their opponents of insufficient zeal
for peace. This had not cost American lives at the time. But the Cold
War politicians who profited by branding as warmongering the distinction between war and peace, between victory and defeat, did so
even as they were sending fellow Americans into harm's way.

Ronald Reagan's rhetorical restoration of the concepts of victory and peace during the 1980s hardly affected real US policy.
As Reagan came to office, Iran released American diplomats it
had held for over a year, but continued to occupy the US Embassy
it had taken. How should America deal with that textbook act
of war in a way that would discourage further acts of war? The
Reagan team cut short that discussion, thus granting Iran a victory and encouraging a generation of anti-American terrorism in

the Middle East. In 1982, it sent the Marines to Lebanon, as they had been sent to Vietnam, to help a friendly government establish peace against a common enemy—in this case, Syria. But the troops were sent without a plan for imposing that peace. After Secretary of State George Shultz had boasted: "The Marines can take care of themselves,"[3] Syrian proxies blew up 243 of them. Peace on the cheap proved as impossible as ever. The administration cut short congressional discussions about what a proper squaring of accounts with Syria might be, and withdrew the blooded and defeated Marines.

Notwithstanding the Soviet Union's collapse (and hence the disappearance of the excuse that half-baking America's commitments serves to avoid "mutual annihilation"), the century's dominant pattern continued: In Somalia in 1992–93, our ruling class committed American troops against what FDR had called "ancient evils, ancient ills," to . . . well, to be withdrawn blooded and defeated. In 1994–97, our ruling class again committed American troops to the former Yugoslavia, to establish peace, yes, peace—but not for America, rather among its ever-warring religious communities. It failed as always to get beyond a ceasefire (the Dayton Accords of 1996). The practice of half-baking commitments was now "baked-in."

But by then peace for America had long since ceased to be the objective of American statesmanship, and the American people had become accustomed to fruitless, endless, military commitments made on the authority of their betters.

In 1990 Iraq's Saddam Hussein invaded and annexed nearby Kuwait. The US government, which had been romancing Saddam, at first chose to ignore the event and to continue trying to cement his friendship. It made some sense to continue doing that. Then it committed a half-million magnificently equipped troops to trash his army and reverse the invasion. It hoped loudly that winning the battle of Kuwait—*which it misinterpreted as winning a war*—would enable a US-sponsored general "peace process" for the Middle East. But attacking Saddam while making sure that he would not be overthrown made no sense and established no peace. Rather, it made Saddam an implacable enemy, while showing that defying America does not carry lethal consequences.

The Middle East's surmise of the events of 1990–91 ended up being that Saddam had withstood America's full might, then to spit in its face. Saddam quickly became the Middle East's paladin of anti-Americanism and a proud sponsor of all manner of terrorism. Consequently, America's subsequent "Middle East Peace Process" became a vehicle for Arab potentates' demands on an America they increasingly disrespected. Our ruling class never had read Machiavelli: "enemies are to be caressed or extinguished." That is, *if you want peace, never do your enemy a little harm.*

The Bush (41) administration feared that, once American troops were committed, US public opinion would demand Saddam's overthrow. It precluded such unsophisticated demands by setting the Gulf War's parameters in cooperation with the UN and with the governments of the Arab world that joined the venture. Surely, these sophisticates knew better than ordinary Americans. As it turned out, their combined wisdom left the American people with less peace than before.

Progressives and Their Children

Another fountainhead of our ruling class's reticence to think about enforcing America's peace vis-à-vis peoples of the so-called "Third World" is that this mass of post-colonial states is substantially an American invention. President John F. Kennedy had bet America's position in the world on faith that "Third World" revolutionaries would be grateful for US help against Britain and France. Paul Johnson's *Modern Times: The World from the Twenties to the Nineties,* especially the chapter titled "The Bandung Generation," gives a good account of how America's ruling class fostered decolonization, from Africa's West coast to the East coast of Asia during the 1950s and 60s. It did so through official diplomacy and "grey" and "black" activities by such as the Ford Foundation in league with the CIA.

The CIA in particular imagines to this day that it has privileged relations with any number of the "third world" elites whose early careers it fostered and whom it continues to subsidize. The fact that many such elites turned into blood enemies of America (Saddam

Hussein, Yasser Arafat, and Franz Fanon are but the best known) is less important than that Americans of the realist, liberal internationalist, and neoconservative schools, each for its own reasons, look upon "Third World" elites as potential images of themselves. Moreover, they continue to view "Third World" causes favorably. Our ruling class forgot or never read Edward Gibbon's and Montesquieu's description of how the Roman Empire's subsidies of barbarian tribes produced mainly the demand for more subsidies, and contempt for the Romans.

What the world learned from our ruling class's commitment of American lives and treasure while *unwilling in principle* to commit to America's peace and *reluctant in principle* to submit to the American people's judgment, bode ill for the future. By the turn of our century, terrorists from the Muslim world and the governments that had educated them, that shelter them, and in some cases employ them, had a pretty accurate idea of what they could expect from the US government in retaliation for striking America.

19

Peacekeeping vs. Peace

The American ruling class's consensus that it has the right and duty to prod, if not to shove, foreigners up the evolutionary ladder—and lesser Americans as well—led the US government to engage foreign peoples as deeply as many traditional empires had, and exposed the American people to the ills normally attendant to empire-keeping. This has deep Darwinist roots. As we have seen, during the Mexican War of 1846–48 some progressive-minded Northerners were as convinced of their duty to dominate Mexicans for their benefit as Southern slaveholders were of theirs to do that to Negroes. The architects of post-Civil War Reconstruction wanted to uplift the South's blacks while teaching Southern whites a lesson—America's first venture in "nation-building." Turn-of-the-century imperialists wanted to take on the global "white man's burden." Woodrow Wilson cast the Great War as mankind's final struggle for perpetual peace, and invaded Mexico to "teach them to elect good men." Since World War II, our ruling class has imagined itself quieting mankind's quarrels and leading humanity to victory over poverty, disease, and ignorance. *progress*

Inertial Empire

The Cold War's consensus on foreign policy amounted to this: To keep Communists from "fishing in troubled waters," America must prevent as many as possible of the globe's quarrels from turning violent. It must also provide "international assistance" (*né* "foreign aid") to guide the mass of backward humanity's social development. While the Soviet Empire lasted, our ruling class's interference in other peoples' business was limited to the single issue of alignment in the struggle against the Soviet Union. After the Cold War, the inertial force of habit and an environment of reduced risk led to deeper involvement in more countries with less and less force, more and more reflexively. Thus did the ruling class further hazard America's peace.

Because the American people recoil at the notion of being "the world's policemen," few argued explicitly that the United States should take on Great Britain's former role in maintaining global order. "Imperialist!" had been the Soviet Union's slander upon America. Imperialism runs against the American people's grain. Nevertheless, by the turn of our century American troops were deployed in some 150 countries. Even when not engaged directly in military operations, US military and civilian personnel advise governments in Colombia and other places engaged in civil war. American diplomacy is the hinge of hot and cold wars in the Middle East and East Asia. Elsewhere, the US government is involved—if only verbally—in controversies of deadly importance. All agree that the American people want no part of empire. But (so goes the consensus) great power requires exercising imperial responsibility; if the great power shuns responsibility, the world will slide into chaos, and the great power will lose the peace.

But, by 2012, America's deep involvement had led to the black flag of the Muslim jihadist movement flying over four US embassies as rioters besieged two dozen more, and terrorism had become an American domestic reality.

In short: *America neither wages war in the dictionary meaning of the term nor enjoys peace. This is what so often happens to imperial powers: because they seek to manage peoples rather than to eliminate enemies, they seldom wage real wars. Nor can they ever really be at peace with those they are trying to manage. Eventually, colonial wars come home.* This is the polar opposite of John Quincy Adams's notion that wise foreign policy begins (but does not end) with an attempt to imitate the golden rule: If you want to be left in peace, it really does help to leave others in peace, too.

The elite consensus that reversed the founding generation's commonsense is as shallow as it is broad. Our foreign policy establishment, composed of liberal internationalist, realist, and neoconservative wings, is unanimous that America should lead the world and that the world yearns for their particular brand of leadership. But its components' prescriptions, lacking as they do the capacity to compel results, result in more trouble than peace.

During the Cold War, anti-Communists were proud that America radiated some of its domestic peace, freedom, and prosperity from Helsinki to Hong Kong—the *Pax Americana*. Anti-Communists wanted to "make tyranny tremble" because, it just so happened, the principal threats to America's interests were a species of tyrants, Communists. The widespread belief that opposing *these* tyrants was good for America and for the world brought together Americans whose primary concern was with what George Washington had called "our interest guided by justice" and *some* of those who, following Woodrow Wilson, imagined that there was no difference between the interests of Americans and those of mankind in general.

But other Wilsonians were anti-anti-Communists. Their mindset was mirrored by William Appleman Williams's *The Tragedy of American Diplomacy* (1959). They wanted America engaged in the Cold War, all right—but on the other side. Eventually, this New Left's thinking spread throughout America's foreign policy establishment.

The Cold War's immediacy helped to ease our ruling class into commitments intentionally fuzzy to cover the often-contradictory purposes of its various sectors.

Dramatis Personae

Liberal Internationalists believe that America must play a Progressive role in the world, and resent bitterly the American people's unwillingness to do that. This position's most concise statement in our time, Arthur M. Schlesinger, Jr.'s 1995 *Foreign Affairs* article, "Back to the Womb? Isolationism's Renewed Threat" argued that multilateral institutions embody the world mind—that is, the preferences of people like himself. Americans must cheerfully support the United Nations, engage in peacekeeping missions, increase foreign aid, serve multilateral causes.

Schlesinger's point was *not* that Americans should overthrow the world's bad guys, but rather that Americans should expose themselves to danger as part of largely peaceful multilateral efforts at progressive reform—however the World Mind (i.e., US Liberal Internationalists and their far-flung friends) might define that.

Neoconservatism is nearly a mirror image of Schlesinger's liberalism. Joshua Muravchik's 1996 *Foreign Affairs* article "The Imperative of American Leadership: A Challenge to Neo-Isolationism" also inveighs against the American people's preference for minding their own business. But Muravchik and neoconservatives believe that Americans have a duty to "rule—or lead—others" because "there is no authority higher than America. . . . In short, America must accept the role of world leader." America freed the world from the Soviets, and only it has what it takes to help people free themselves from the remaining bad guys. We Americans have the moral legitimacy that comes from disinterestedness, and the power; we should also have the will. As William Kristol and Robert Kagan put it in the 1996 *Foreign Affairs* article "Toward a Neo-Reaganite Foreign Policy," declining responsibility for "the peace and security of the international order . . . becomes in practice a policy of cowardice and dishonor." This position amounts to the "benign," "temporary," "imperialism" advocated by Norman Podhoretz.

Neoconservatives are more willing than liberals to use some force to benefit mankind. But, like liberals, they cannot imagine people to people wars because, like liberals, they hardly consider the possibility that foreigners' resistance to our leadership might take more to overcome than it would be good for us to exert.

An older realism sees the world in need of a mere "sheriff," and Americans wearing the star, but acknowledges that the "sheriffing" must actually serve US interests. Colin Gray argued (*The Sheriff: America's Defense of the New World Order*, 2004) that the world is lucky, and that all states may benefit if non-predatory America quashes the world's disrupters. Gray has no doubt that anti-US terrorism is a price that Americans must pay for playing what he considers America's proper role in the Middle East. Yet Gray writes that the US government should play sheriff only to the extent that the price for doing so is kept low because, if the United States does not serve itself through sheriffing, its career as sheriff will be brief indeed. Realists, however, have seldom paid attention to how much war America must suffer just to *try* providing for others' peace.

Modern realists William Odom and Robert Dujarric argued in *America's Inadvertent Empire* (2004) that America must "lead the world" because what the authors call "American institutions" fit America for the job. These they call "patterns, rules and practices most often manifested in organizations—political, social, and economic— . . . they also include ideologies, which are made up of beliefs—religious, moral and cultural—that individuals use to explain and rationalize the world around them." English translation: Americans are the only modern people so morally grounded that they are willing to give their lives for causes they deem just.

Our Soul at Stake

Yet while the authors do not describe what the source of that morality might be, what undermines it, and what preserves it, they make clear that bending US policy to reflect the interest of the countries they call the empire's "full stakeholders" might sacrifice America's soul. That is not news. John Quincy Adams had warned that an America engaged in others' business "would be no longer the ruler of her own soul."

Niall Ferguson's *Colossus: The Rise and Fall of American Empire* (2004) abstracts from souls. For Ferguson, all human activity has the same objective purpose: domination. Ferguson's America is necessarily imperialistic because it is big and pervasive. A British subject, Ferguson asserts: (1) Americans have always exacerbated their imperial grasping by hypocrisy; (2) Americans are insufficiently experienced in hypocrisy and must learn it from the masters; and (3) Americans deserve the troubles they bring on themselves, because they are both stupid and usually on the wrong side of things. Therefore, he blames the United States for terrorism: the United States helped "Israel establish military superiority over the Arab counties, *forcing* the Palestinians to resort to terrorism . . ."[1] (emphasis added). He laments: why can't the Americans do empire with style—the way the British did, without American nonsense about right and wrong?

In short, Ferguson likes imperialism, but not imperial America because he detests America's culture, which he calls a "novel

Protestant-Deist-Catholic-Jewish fusion."[2] It does not occur to him that, without America's peculiar culture, there would be no American power—that all depends on the character of souls.

A Loose Grip on the Subject

Now for the reality: Today's American empire began in October 1956, when America's foreign policy establishment sided against Britain's and France's forceful protection of their property in the Suez Canal, which Egypt's new Gamal Abdel Nasser regime had nationalized. These Americans (especially at the CIA), who thought of themselves as "the real revolutionaries," believed that they could resolve the quarrels of what would become known as "the Third World," and *guide its administration and development*—an imperialist commitment that could be fulfilled only in the absence of significant opposition. They believed there would be next to no opposition.

But because opposition was always there, efforts to fulfill such commitments abroad produced inconclusive military engagements. At home, they upset the balance among the elements of America's culture.

Already in 1953 the US government had decided to create a surrogate in the Middle East by shaping Iran's monarchy to CIA standards. Under the guidance and with the help of the CIA's Liberal Internationalist experts, Iran's Shah Westernized his country, removing as much of Shia Islam's symbols and sustenance as he could. But this "white revolution," as his American advisers called it, made the Shah so unpopular that the black-robed Ayatollah Khomeini easily mustered mobs against him—and against America.

Desperate for a *point d'appui* in the Middle East after the Shah's overthrow by the Shia, America's liberals, neoconservatives, and realists imagined a Sunni-based, anti-Shia alliance composed of the Saudi monarchy (which ruled on behalf of the radical Wahabi sect) and of Iraq—Iran's historic enemy, where secular Sunni Saddam Hussein ruled a Shia majority on behalf of a Sunni minority. This US project also included several Gulf sheikdoms where the Shia are under Sunni rule. Our establishment did not imagine either that Saddam, whom the CIA had helped to power would pay no attention to the role that Americans envisaged for him, or that Iran would become the focus of hope for the world's Shia. Both happened.

Our ruling class was surprised that Saddam took the first opportunity to aggrandize himself at the expense of his nearest neighbors—Kuwait and Saudi Arabia—Sunni-ruled though they are. Then, our statesmen convinced themselves that pushing Saddam back to his own borders (what they called the Gulf War of 1991) would cement their leadership of the Middle East (especially among the Arabs whose chestnuts America had pulled from the fire) and enable them to settle its disputes, including the perennial Arab-Israeli conflict. Reality baffled our bipartisan ruling class. Again.

They could not understand why, after 1991, these Arab states became more anti-American, more supportive of terrorism than ever, why the 1990s saw a crescendo of anti-American terrorist attacks, why terrorists cited specifically the US actions against Iraq as the justification for their outrages: the bombings of US embassies, the near sinking of the USS *Cole,* and 9/11 itself. Osama bin Laden's anti-American *fatwa* of 1996 deals disproportionately with Iraq. In short, they did not understand that the events of 1990–91 had increased hate for, decreased fear of, and hence decreased respect for, America.

US policy toward Egypt from 1956 to our time may be summed up as "futile attempts to purchase its rulers' favor." Colonel Gamal Nasser had taken power in Egypt in 1953 with support from the Muslim Brotherhood and money from the CIA. But, thereafter, he did not need the latter to suppress the former. Just gallows and jails. The Americans offered Nasser liberal schemes of economic development. But Nasser wanted weapons to attack Israel, and got them from the Soviets. In 1972, his successors felt the Soviet grip tightening, and began to turn westward. They began accepting some $2 billion per year from the United States in exchange for promises not to attack Israel—which they were not about to do, having recently lost yet another war to that country.

Americans thought that the money would also buy liberal socioeconomic development, a measure of democracy, and moderation too. But Egypt's military rulers kept the cash for themselves. Meanwhile they diverted outward the ever-growing Muslim Brotherhood's anger. More and more, Egypt became the main intellectual source of Sunni Islam's terrorism against America to the point that, in 2012, when the Brotherhood replaced the military, its first demand was that America free the Egyptian cleric convicted of the 1993 attack on the World Trade Center. Yet by 2013, as the Brotherhood's misrule led to the military's renewed repression of it, the US government had so identified itself with the Brotherhood as to share in the Egyptian people's revulsion against it.

By 2012, Iran's Islamic Republic had erased any remaining doubt about the self-defeating nature of our ruling class's engagement with the Third World. It is no exaggeration to state that every administration from Bill Clinton's to Barack Obama's used every tool, every approach of every part of the US foreign policy establishment to prevent, dissuade, even just to delay Iran's acquisition of nuclear weapons. But the liberals' offers of aid did not persuade Iran's mullahs to prefer joining "the international community" to having nukes. Nor did the neoconservatives' talk of "regime change," coupled with empty threats of "surgical strikes," do the trick. The realists' economic "smart sanctions" also proved unequal to this consensus US establishment objective.

In sum, the US foreign policy establishment's several factions speak in inherently meaningless terms such as "security assistance," "democratic support," "bombing," or "boots on the ground." Abstract language helps them to avoid explaining, above all to themselves, why their recipes should produce the results they expect—just what *this* alignment with a foreign faction, *those* subsidies, the destruction of *these* bombing targets or the killing of *those* individuals, or "boots on the ground," would do to secure the peace Americans want. Having lost the habit of connecting ends and means, each faction talks loudly and then executes policies that discredit and dispirit America. Thus has America begun to suffer the fate of empires.

Souls, Forgotten and Lost

Rudyard Kipling's 1897 warning to his countrymen as they celebrated their empire is worth recalling:

God of our fathers, known of old—
Lord of our far-flung battle-line—
Beneath whose awful Hand we hold
Dominion over palm and pine—
Lord God of Hosts, be with us yet,
Lest we forget, lest we forget! . . .

Far-call'd our navies melt away—
On dune and headland sinks the fire—
Lo, all our pomp of yesterday
Is one with Nineveh and Tyre!
Judge of the Nations, spare us yet,
Lest we forget, lest we forget!

If, drunk with sight of power, we loose
Wild tongues that have not Thee in awe—
Such boasting as the Gentiles use
Or lesser breeds without the Law—
Lord God of Hosts, be with us yet,
Lest we forget, lest we forget!

For heathen heart that puts her trust
In reeking tube and iron shard—
All valiant dust that builds on dust,
And guarding calls not Thee to guard—
For frantic boast and foolish word,
Thy Mercy on Thy People, Lord!

A poet, Kipling did not specify what Britain's ruling class would "forget" by watching over "palm and pine." But always and everywhere, immersion in unessential things obscures the essential ones. Imperial Britain suffered more than its forces' wear on "dune and headlands." Like Athens and Rome, like other self-governing powers that lost their character by ruling others, Britain forgot how and why it had ruled itself.

In short, because empire-keeping sets up countless confrontations with alien ways, it forces the imperialist to choose again and again between forcefully imposing his ways on others or having others' imposed on him. The imperialist fancies he can evade the choice and keep his compass. But empire cripples first his judgment, and then his soul.

Britain's imperial career began to end in 1919 in the city of Amritsar, India, when a British officer read "the Riot Act" to a mob of some 15,000, then killed 379 and wounded 1,100. A half-century earlier, British public opinion had noted such events as evidence that Britain was imposing civilization on savages. A story, likely apocryphal, illustrates that earlier era's mindset. An Indian protesting the viceroy's ban against the suttee (burning widows on their husbands' funeral pyres) as "our custom, our religion" is said to have received the following reply from a British officer: "We too have a custom driven by our religion regarding men who burn women. We hang them." But, by 1919, British society was no longer sure what it would tolerate, what not, which things are worthy of toleration and which things are not.

In our time, British society has become so tolerant of intolerant peoples that it tolerates less and less its own members' criticism of the intolerant ones. In the resulting confusion, the moral qualities that had made Britain the school of Europe, if not of the world, vanished quite as much as those of Athens had vanished through the Peloponnesian War that the Athenian empire had engendered. America seems to be following suit.

In twenty-first-century America, the ruling class consensus appears to be that many, prolonged, inconclusive involvements all over the world are a permanent, sustainable feature of America's life. But these adventures are unsustainable above all because they lead America to forget what it is about. In 2012 Afghan troops mingled with Americans were outraged that the infidels sometimes walked in front of them during prayers, and demanded that the infidels wear surgical gloves when handling the Koran, while the Americans were revolted by the Afghans' use of street waifs as "dancing boys" kept for anal intercourse, as well as by their torturing dogs for fun. The Pentagon's answer was to train US soldiers to tolerate the Afghans' ways. It did not occur to US officials to insist that the Afghans respect the Americans' sensibilities.

The following is exemplar of the contrary. After 30 US troops died when their helicopter was shot down over Afghanistan on August 6, 2011, their US military funeral featured an imam who chanted over the coffins (in Arabic): "The companions of the fire [that is, these dead infidels] are not equal with the companions of heaven, who are the winners. We present their fate to the people so that they may convert. . . ." If indeed America's relations with the world are a struggle for hearts, minds, and souls, we may ask whose heart, mind, and soul had done what to whose?

Islam, by Default

Throughout the Muslim world there is no high-level dissent from the proposition that Muslims have the right and duty to kill *any* infidels, because *some* infidels have disrespected Islam, and no acknowledgment of the infidels' right to their own ways when these conflict with Islam. In 2013 Muslim mobs and death squads burned and blasted Christian churches throughout the Middle East and Africa. Whereas in 1950 Christians amounted to one-fifth of the Middle East's population, by 2013 that population had been reduced to two in a hundred.

In 2012 Muslim leaders cited an anti-Muslim video made in the United States as good cause for anti-American violence. The presidents of Egypt and Turkey (both of the Muslim Brotherhood) demanded that the US government act against any Americans who *they* say defame Islam. They argued that we who indulge our right to free speech cannot complain when Muslims indulge their right to burn our embassies and kill our diplomats. In other words: if you Americans want to feel safe, you must make sure not to offend us. They felt safe demanding this because our ruling class seems not to have thought of forcing respect for ordinary Americans' safety and sensibilities—sensibilities that the ruling class shares less and less.

The mindset of America's ruling class may be seen by its media's definition as "hate speech" of a billboard in New York subways that said, "In any war between the civilized man and the savage, support the civilized man. Support Israel. Defeat jihad." Without benefit of full-dress argument, *it judged the mere apposition of civilization and jihad to be more hateful than jihad.* Thus also President Barack Obama, speaking to the United Nations, condemned *in equal terms* Americans who insult Muslims, and Muslims who burn and kill Americans. His administration also ordered the offending video maker's imprisonment. Hate speech, you know.

However, none of those sensibilities kept the ruling class from denouncing its opponents in domestic fiscal struggles as "jihadists," as "hostage takers," as "terrorists with bombs strapped to their chests."

As Americans adopt clashing civilizational sensibilities, America's public life is increasingly characterized by groups that struggle to stigmatize each other as intolerable haters. Peace at home becomes as problematic as peace abroad.

Unlike America's founders, unlike their forbears in the Cold War's early years, today's ruling class does not think about what America would have to do, and above all *to be,* for Americans to live peacefully among ourselves and among alien peoples. Our century's foreign engagements of the imperial kind have abetted this willful forgetting of the basis of our peace.

20

The War on Peace

The "war on terror" became a war on peace itself because American statesmen, increasingly alienated from America's culture, conceived of what they were doing in terms invented to skirt the cultural basis of terrorism. That is why these terms guarantee endless strife.

The Muslim world does not live in peace, domestic or international. The bedrock Koranic principle—that *dar al-Islam* is the realm of peace, whereas the rest of mankind lives in *dar al-harb*, the place of war—is the reverse of reality. The deepest reason for this, Sunni Islam's theological rejection of reason in the mutawalite controversy of the eleventh century, is beyond our scope.

In modern times, the Muslim world began exporting its warfare beginning in the late 1960s. Our bipartisan ruling class did not take it seriously, treating even Iran's 1979 seizure of the US Embassy and diplomats—a textbook act of war—as a minor irritation. It refused to confront the fact that its conception of a peaceful post-colonial world is flawed, that the Muslim world in particular would present Western civilization with deadly multidimensional challenges that reach within our own body politic.

What War, on Whom?

The events of 9/11, however, looked too much like war to be treated lightly. Still, our ruling class refused to consider what establishing America's peace would take. President George W. Bush personally declared war: *sort of but not really, on no one in particular.* What he meant is beside the point of what followed, namely a lot of shooting and spending that led not to peace but to the American people's further alienation from peace, from their government, and from one another.

What did anyone expect? Ordinary Americans expected what President Bush promised on September 20, 2001, that US military operations post-9/11 would yield the heads, and surely the tails, of any and all who had bloodied Americans or had enabled terrorists. Americans wanted to exterminate mankind's vermin as vehemently as had John Quincy Adams.

Although, by 2001, few alive remembered life as free as it had been before terrorism's onset in the late 1960s, all wanted to live in peace at least as trouble-free as on September 10. But our ruling class concluded that America would have to change—and not for the better. Senator Phil Gramm's *cri de coeur* "I don't want to change the way we live!" reflected the popular view, but proved to be contrarian. Our ruling class rushed above all to change American people's lives. Peace was the first casualty.

The *title* of the initial US military operation, "Enduring Freedom," encapsulated the people's interest. But the *substance* did not. No US military operation in the "war on terror" was ever formulated to restore any freedom, to end any problem.

The Congress never debated alternatives, nor settled on a course of action. Instead, the "war" policy, set by the executive branch of government, was the geometric resultant of the ruling class's clashing intramural preferences. Its members doubled down on what they had been thinking and doing, never reasonably connecting means ad hoc to ends. *Whatever the American ruling class was thinking, it was not thinking about establishing peace or about maintaining the way we live.* Without explanation, it sacrificed both piecemeal to "the war," slipped into the habit acquired during the Cold War of regarding the struggle as eternal, and settled down to the pleasure and profit of managing it.

The Muslim World

Understanding our ruling class's dysfunctional war requires keeping in mind its misunderstanding of the Muslim world and of America itself. Aggressively ignorant of all religion, it took for granted that

Islam was even more a relic of the past than Christianity. Turkey's defeat in World War I had ended the Ottoman Caliphate. Mustafa Kemal, known thereafter as Atatürk (father of Turks), had forcefully secularized its Turkish home. For generations thereafter, polite opinion deemed unworthy of notice the Muslim response, the Muslim Brotherhood, founded by Hassan al-Banna, an obscure Egyptian.

Our ruling class supported the Muslim world's secular revolutionaries as if they were imitators of Atatürk, and as if they were inherently friendly to America. Neither was true. Thus, when speaking to CIA Director Allen Dulles (1953–1961), Secretary of State John Foster Dulles used to refer to Egypt's dictator Gamal Abdel Nasser as "your colonel," because the CIA had had a big hand in bringing him to power. CIA was also present at Nasser's creation of Yasser Arafat's *Fatah* (1959), which became the Palestine Liberation Organization (PLO) and which the US government later helped to transmute into the Palestinian Authority (PLA). In 1982, when Israel's invasion of Lebanon had placed Lebanese Christian forces in the position physically to annihilate the PLO, the CIA prevailed in US government councils to save Arafat and hundreds of PLO cadres, transferring them to Tunisia on US ships.

The fact that this happened a decade *after* the PLO had murdered Israeli athletes at the Munich Olympics, *after* it had assassinated a US ambassador, the fact that the US government continues to subsidize the PLA, shows how impervious to reality have been the hopes that our ruling class continues to place on people like Arafat. The CIA also started Saddam Hussein's career in 1959, and helped bring to power the secular Ba'ath Party that ruled Iraq and Syria in alliance with America's enemies.

Ignorance about Islamist revolutionaries matched our ruling class's ignorance about secular ones. Islam's day had never passed. Islam is, and cannot but remain, the only authoritative standard of good and evil, right and wrong, available to the Muslim world. Whereas the Ottoman Caliphs had developed an increasingly Western outlook over centuries and had the authority to interpret Islamic law, the Sharia, as best suited them, the underground Brotherhood had no authority but the Sharia and no goal but to reverse the Atatürk revolution. Meanwhile Saudi Arabia's native Wahabi movement grew in parallel, fed by oil money. Thus, roughly in proportion to Western civilization's evident weakening and to the failure of the Muslim world's westernizing regimes to embody appealing cultural models, Islam and its law reasserted themselves from the Atlantic to the Pacific in newly militant ways.

By 2012, Atatürk was history, and a version of Islam had reconquered its native region as well as energized violent dissidence within Europe and America itself. By 2012, Turkey itself was ruled by a party affiliated with the Brotherhood, which jailed the generals who had guarded Atatürk's revolution. It re-Isamized the state apparatus, and laid the groundwork for an Islamic dictatorship. In Egypt, a Brotherhood dictator had replaced Nasser's military heirs. These turned the tables a year later. But the Brotherhood remained the only alternative.

Western polling organizations in the Muslim world confirm that the Muslim masses' primary complaint against westernizing rulers is lack of Islamic, anti-Western commitment—neither brutality nor kleptocracy, much less authoritarianism. They accept Saudi Arabia's regime—which defines authoritarianism and kleptocracy—because it embodies the Wahabi sect at home and funds the Muslim Brotherhood abroad. Our ruling class has yet to catch on that this is problematic for our peace.

It did not grasp that the Ayatollah Khomeini's 1979 overthrow of Iran's Shah was a rejection of Western civilization. Nor did it see that such secularists as Saddam Hussein who styled themselves as champions of Islam were helping to redefine Islam in anti-Western terms. Nor did it grasp that Islam's perennial internal struggles are being won by its most violent elements—the Wahabis and the Muslim Brotherhood. The Obama administration officially reported to Congress that the Brotherhood is a "mostly secular" organization. Some at CIA even saw the Muslim Brotherhood as "the Muslim equivalent of Europe's Christian Democratic parties." Our culturally, historically illiterate ruling class missed the fact that a whole civilization was being mobilized against America and that this is a big, multidimensional problem.

How big is the problem? Consider: Islamic civilization had been the West's biggest problem from the eighth century AD until 1683, when

Poland's king Jan Sobieski destroyed the Muslim host at the gates of Vienna. (What if his cavalry charge had failed, or if the 732 AD Battle of Tours had gone the way that the battle of Constantinople went in 1453?) Even so, Muslim pirates continued to terrorize the Mediterranean, to take Christian slaves, and to prey on commerce until France subdued North Africa in 1830. In the extraordinary period between 1830 and the 1960s, the Muslim world posed no problem. Now the problem is back. Might events on the scale of 723, 1683, or 1830 be required to restore our peace vis-à-vis that world? Perhaps not. But then what *would* it take? This question is the touchstone of seriousness.

Our ruling class skirts serious answers and doubles down on its own fancies, unable to see that the response to a civilizational challenge must begin by strengthening our own civilization.

What Is America About?

Whereas, at the outset of the Cold War, our leaders more or less came together for a crucial while on the need to reaffirm the American people's profession and practice of Judeo-Christian civilization—recall Will Herberg's *Protestant-Catholic-Jew* (1955)—the ruling class's response to 9/11 seemed to confirm the Muslim world's indictment of the West for cultural nihilism. Thus US media, US diplomacy, and US armed forces abroad promote the same recipe of secularism and sex roles that have been the substance of its *Kulturkampf* at home. Our ruling class tries to impose its preferred "human rights" on backward foreigners out of the same sense of intellectual-moral entitlement by which it bids to reform backward Americans. Secretary of State Hilary Clinton said: "Gay rights are human rights, and human rights are gay rights." Thus accordingly, every year, all US embassies observe "gay pride month," including rebukes to the locals who dissent from its premises—in the name of the American people. For example, while Pakistani law imposes two years' imprisonment for sexual acts "against the order of nature," the US Embassy publicly "stands with" those who violate that law.

No surprise, then, that the Muslim world's common-currency, by no means confined to "extremists," is that America embodies and exports godlessness, immorality, the dissolution of families—that America is mankind's nuisance, if not the enemy of all good things. Indeed, a poll of Afghanistan's Taliban fighters confirmed that they were motivated principally by foreigners' attempts to impose an alien way of life upon them. Our ruling class counters that terrorism and violence in general are the consequence of insufficient secularization, of moral fixations, and of rigidity in gender roles. Hence America must fight to break down these mores.

So, while the Muslim world was always the enemy of Judeo-Christian civilization, it is twice fiercely the enemy of aggressively post-Christian America.

Al-Qaeda?

Yet, 9/11 demanded that that the US government do *something* in or about the Muslim world. But what? And what would that achieve? The president, the government, the media, and, hence, public opinion accepted without question the CIA's definition of responsibility for 9/11 and, by implication, for terrorism in general: Osama bin Laden's al-Qaeda. This was a motley crew of some 200, mostly Arabs, mostly useless, who had joined Osama in Afghanistan in the mid-1980s to fight the Soviets, had followed him in 1989 to Saudi Arabia and Sudan, and then followed him back again in 1996—on a Russian aircraft rumored to have been brokered in Iraq.

Imputing responsibility to these so called "Afghan Arabs," *persons extraneous to the Muslim world's ruling class,* with which the US government has what it considers good relations, delimited what US policymakers considered to be the problem. Conveniently, this exonerated the Muslim world's most influential people and diverted attention from weighty religious-cultural factors. But tailoring US actions to that narrowly defined problem guaranteed that no amount of effort would bring peace.

Reflexively, the US government labeled any and all persons against whom it directed the "war on terror's" operations as "al-Qaeda." It considered terrorism by non-"Afghan Arabs" as evidence that al-Qaeda had *"metastasized" or "franchised"*—metaphors that befog the question. Followed by academics who should know better and by a lazy press, the government reasoned that since al-Qaeda does x, y, and z, therefore whoever does x, y, and z must be al-Qaeda, however extraneous they be to "Afghan Arabs." So, people from Africa to Ruritania intent on terrorizing grasped that calling themselves al-Qaeda is something of a "force multiplier." As Muslims born or converted in America and Europe radicalized themselves and committed terrorist acts, our ruling class debated fruitlessly whether they were "al-Qaeda" or not without reconsidering what use of the term adds to or subtracts from our understanding of the phenomenon.

In sum, our ruling class's construct of al-Qaeda is emblematic of its lack of intellectual rigor in the service of escapism.

The Bush and Obama administrations seem to have assumed, privately as well as publicly, that eliminating bin Laden and his bunch would deliver peace from terrorism. They never explained how the demise of this set of "rogues" would achieve that result. But the notion that Osama, *or any set of "rogues,"* is the proximate (never mind the ultimate) cause of anti-American terrorism was always patent nonsense. Osama had proved irrelevant a decade before he died in 2011. *That death changed nothing.*

Even as al-Qaeda waned post-9/11 (estimates of the number of "Afghan Arabs" alive and at large in 2013 ranged around two dozen), terrorism continued to wax while what was left of respect for America turned to contempt: Whereas, on the night of 9/11, Muslim governments had quickly dispersed the crowds celebrating the carnage lest the sight provoke America, on September 11, 2012, governments through much of the Muslim world were neutral or complicit in murderous mob attacks on US Embassies in their capitals, as the marshaled mobs shouted: "Obama, Obama, there are a billion Osamas." Indeed.

America, bloodied and thrashing like a wounded animal, was drawing predators small and large at home as well as abroad.

The Logic of Peace and War

The collective wisdom of our bipartisan "best and brightest" went so wrong, because it spurned the natural logic of peace and war.

By logic, defining military operations follows tightly from defining the ends that the operations are to serve. By nature, this work of definition consists of the deliberative concatenation of ends and means. This is a legislative function (intellectually though not necessarily organizationally). As such, it requires confronting alternatives and admits of no intellectual shortcuts: *What is the problem? Will these operations' success restore the peace?* Military forces are good for killing people. Killing people can serve to eliminate troubles. *The test of military operations is whether, if and when they are successful at killing the people intended to be killed, the troubles persist or not.* If the troubles do persist, it means perforce that the people who were killed were less troublesome than those left alive, and hence that the military operations were ill conceived. It means that those who defined the operations proved themselves unworthy of their jobs.

US military operations in 2001–2003 killed any number of people in Afghanistan and Iraq in the process of overthrowing those countries' governments. These deaths naturally reduced America's problems to some extent. But our ruling class neither understood what opportunities these operations had produced nor could it draw benefit from them. Because it never grasped the problems, it had merely thrown effort at them. Thereafter, groping, it applied to both countries what had become its default remedy: sociopolitical "nation-building" shielded by military forces. This imperial negation of the distinction between war and peace fed new conflicts with mostly new enemies and without logical end.

This is how the "war on terror" produced more war than peace.

What Is the Obstacle to Peace?

By November 2001, US forces had provided air support to Afghanistan's Northern Alliance of Tajik and Uzbek tribes, enabling them to win their long-running war against the Pashtun tribes of Southern and Eastern Afghanistan and their Taliban government. In the Afghan fashion, most Pashtun cast off the Taliban label, switched sides, and sold their "Afghan Arab" auxiliaries to the United States, which shipped them to Guantanamo Bay prison. Though there is no evidence that anyone killed or captured in Afghanistan had a role in the September 11 attacks, and no one suggested that any significant proportion of the leaders or followers of anti-American terrorism were killed, or that the US invasion had defeated hopes for the causes that terrorists serve, the US operation did serve peace by placing the US government in the position to warn Middle Eastern governments that they might expect the same fate as the Taliban, if any anti-US terrorism came from within the places they control.

Our ruling class gave no such warnings. Although most realized that, *pace* the CIA, there was more to the terrorist problem than the "Afghan Arabs," that anti-American terrorism had long predated 9/11 and al-Qaeda, and that as Thomas Friedman put it, "98 percent of terrorism is what governments want to happen or let happen," our ruling class was loath to discuss what the problem to be solved might be. It did not ask: "what is the obstacle to peace?"

In the absence of a good answer to that question, no military operations make sense.

In 2002, the ruling class did not ask those questions because its several factions defined the "war on terror" according to their international preferences and above all according to their own domestic political identities. It is no coincidence that former anti-anti-Communists were now anti-anti-Muslim, and vice versa. The CIA and State Department wanted to shield their "Third World" favorites from the American people's wrath. As during the Cold War, "Progressives" blamed America's troubles on their bellicose fellow citizens. So they pressed to confine antiterrorist operations to further efforts to capture bin Laden and any Afghan Arab or Taliban who remained on the loose. They did not argue that this would bring peace, but rather that this exclusive focus would bring the United States closer to the several Arab governments. This was less a strategy than a reflection of identity.

The Defense Department, for its part, pointed to the fact that most anti-Western terrorists had come from Arab countries, where governments rule with iron hands—Egypt, Syria, Iraq, the Palestinian Authority, and Saudi Arabia, as well as from Iran. It argued that these governments' basic attitudes are the problem, which could be dealt with, if at all, only by *a massive attitude adjustment*. Overthrowing Iraq's Saddam Hussein would begin that adjustment by giving the other governments powerful incentives to curtail incitement and support of terrorism within their borders.

The media translated the interagency argument into partisan terms—Democrats in favor of the State/CIA position, Republicans in favor of the Pentagon. Thus it deepened a preexisting divide within the American body politic and further embittered Americans against one another. The bitterness could only fester unresolved, because the ruling class agreed that the "war on terror's" character should not be set by votes in Congress or by executive branch choices between clear alternatives. So, it ended up being set by intragovernment infighting mostly behind the scenes, featuring competitive leaking to favorite media. The resulting domestic and international incoherence helped make the "war on terror" self-perpetuating—a war on peace.

Iraq War, I & II

George W. Bush adopted all of the contending positions presented to him, and none. At the outset, he sought only the most politically appealing rationale for invading Iraq and overthrowing Saddam. By May 2003, the Iraqi regime that had caused America trouble had been swept away. America had provided an incentive (*potentially lively, had it been pursued*) for good behavior to other Middle Eastern regimes. Regardless of what might have been on George W. Bush's mind when he said that America's military "mission" had been "accomplished" on October 30, 2003, on the USS *Lincoln,* in fact "Iraq War I" had been won. Regardless of what anyone intended or did not intend, the overthrow of an aggressive enemy regime was a (*modest*) gain for peace.

But by then Bush had already begun to squander that gain, because State/CIA and the Saudi king had persuaded him to occupy Iraq indefinitely—that is, to start "Iraq War II." But to do what? Thinly did Bush's rhetoric veil that he never decided.

Everyone except the United States, it seems, had coherent objectives. The Sunni Saudis wanted to preserve the role of Iraq's Sunnis.

Iraq's Sunnis were fighting to keep their privileges. Iraq's Shias wanted to rule the country to avenge themselves against the Sunnis. Iraq's Kurds wanted independence from Arabs, whether Sunni or Shia. All were willing to kill whoever stood in the way of their visions of peace. The moment the Americans took on ruling the country, they got in everybody's way. Hence Americans got killed and maimed on behalf of no objective relevant to America's own peace.

The Bush administration's contention that American troops were fighting terrorists in Iraq who would otherwise be terrorizing American cities was laughable: Why would anyone interested in terrorizing defenseless civilians in Indianapolis take on superbly armed US troops in Fallujah? The Bush team then settled on a less obviously absurd argument: Behind the shield of military occupation, American specialists in nation-building would build Iraq into a united democracy that would not threaten Americans, and whose benign example would transform the Middle East from an incubator of terror into a stabilizing part of the new world order. Alas, by 2005 it was obvious to most sentient beings that Iraq had never been and would not become a nation—never mind a radiator of order.

Iraq War II hardened the divisions between this artificial country's main religious-ethnic groups. The occupation's signature policies, "democracy" and "the surge," also earned America a reputation for fecklessness and dissimulation. Democracy? Far from freeing Iraqis to choose their own government, US viceroys spent most of a decade fruitlessly trying to negate the Shias', Sunnis', and Kurds' democratically expressed mutual antagonism.

Nor did the "surge" defeat anyone. Rather, starting in 2007, the main "surge" policy consisted of turning over to Sunni insurgents the tribal areas into which the Shia were pushing them. Rather than defeating them, the US government began arming them, paying them and protecting their new de facto borders. By the same token, US forces also chose one Shia faction and helped it to defeat its competitors within Shia-majority areas. The results of "the surge" may be called "Shiastan" and "Sunnistan." Before as well as during "the surge," US forces also secured the border of what has become Kurdistan—complete with its own army, flag, and language.

In sum, after a bloody decade, Iraq ended up divided more or less along ancient ethno-religious fault lines but more mutually bitter— though (except the Kurds) united in anti-Americanism—than the United States had found it in May 2003.

The occupation of Iraq also turned Americans against one another, and induced senior US military leaders to violate some of the most basic ethics of the profession of arms: They ordered American troops to operate in replenished minefields, where they lost life and limb. Politicians and generals also imposed "rules of engagement" on the troops that increased the number of dead and wounded, and sloughed off onto subordinates the task of distinguishing friend from foe. Rarely did honor rise above the lower ranks. Americans at home who convinced themselves that some kind of victory had been won should know better. There was neither victory nor peace.

Afghanistan

Similarly, in Afghanistan. By early 2002, Afghanistan had ceased to be any kind of problem for the United States. The Uzbeks and Tajiks had pushed the Pashtun back to their own ethnic areas. All tribes had learned what can happen to those who harbor guests who draw powerful enemies. The several ethnic groups and tribes, left to themselves, were in the process of adjusting to one another as they had for centuries. Almost no Afghans had heard of 9/11. Few had heard of America, and of those who had most thought well of it while the rest feared it. Here, too, America's military squaring of accounts with some of its enemies had made a small but real gain for America's peace.

But the Democratic Party, as a way of attacking "Bush's Iraq war" without seeming unpatriotic, demanded that US troops take a bigger hand in Afghanistan. The Bush team did not have what it takes to reply that further interference in that "graveyard of empires," in the lives of those notoriously xenophobic and bellicose peoples was a recipe for disaster there, and in nearby Pakistan as well. And so, beginning in 2003, the US government began to apply its default "nation-building" recipe: strengthening the central government vis-à-vis the provinces *though this meant disarming the very tribes that had won the victory against the Taliban;* spreading civilian advisers throughout the land bearing inflammatory advice on how to live; making war on anyone who objects. Republicans, not to be outdone in the appearance of patriotism, became champions of the "nation-building" they had despised.

Whatever else happens in Afghanistan, there are now more ferocious persons there with more grudges against America and fewer fears of it than before. But the greater problem is that the US government has contributed to the radicalization of Pakistan. That may well mean more serious threats to our peace than the ones to which we have become accustomed.

By 2013, all but a few of our ruling class had concluded that Iraq-Afghanistan-style "counterinsurgency" (read, nation-building) is never to be repeated, because it proved unsustainable. The ruling consensus on the "war" shifted to "counterterrorism," defined as killing as many persons as possible whom US intelligence designates as members of al-Qaeda or affiliates—whatever that may mean.

Intelligence vs. intelligence

The problem is that, since US intelligence collectors accept what comes their way without too many questions, in practice, the US military simply targets special forces and drone strikes against the persons who their informants designate. The informants, in turn, prepare their offerings to the customer's much-advertised tastes. So, because of US intelligence's aversion to quality control, we can be fairly confident that those killed by counterterrorism operations are the informants' enemies—not so sure whether the people killed had ever heard of America.

The December 30, 2009, deaths by suicide bombing of seven CIA officers in Afghanistan by a man who they had prized as a source of targeting data for over a year gives us a glimpse into this problem's magnitude. How many people US forces had killed at that bomber's behest is an embarrassing secret. The US intelligence system is not set up to protect itself from deception.

In fairness, we must realize how implausible it is to imagine that any intelligence service could deliver the names and addresses of enemy troops, or that the way to end a war is to kill the enemy's rank and file. Our ruling class entertains such notions because it is determined not even to think of the hard things they would have to do to earn respect for America's peace vis-à-vis their counterparts in foreign lands.

Were US officials to shift the "terror war" from killing foot soldiers to constraining foreign rulers, they could use the universal reach of drones to force such potentates to choose between ridding their domains of anti-Americanism and their own sure death. The names and addresses of these persons, the persons whose constraint in pain of death would stop terrorism, are in the public domain. There is no need to seek them out through arcane sources. Hence, intelligence, in its ordinary meaning of commonsense and logic, is essential for dealing with a big problem that consists of mutually reinforcing phenomena: the internal decay of Euro-American civilization and the rise of a vengeful, political Islam. That intelligence is even more lacking, but is beyond our scope.

In sum, by its behavior in Iraq and Afghanistan, our ruling class forced upon American public opinion a version of Gresham's law: Wars that bring no peace drive out ones well calculated to deliver it. Henceforth the US body politic is far less likely than before to support any forceful effort to establish America's peace. What if our ruling class, instead of policing foreign lands and sifting their inhabitants, had confronted foreign rulers with the choice between doing that policing and sifting or having America wage deadly war on them? We will never know.

As our ruling class's fumbling of minor foreign challenges was depleting the American people's reservoir of resolve for dealing with challenges from abroad, serious ones were arising. Russia was re-drawing into itself major pieces of the Soviet Empire, while China was quietly becoming the mistress of the Western Pacific Rim.

21

No Peace at Home

The loss of peace abroad upset the balance between the various elements of life in America, fed domestic strife, and resulted in the loss of peace at home. The need for protection against foreign jihadists and their American imitators occasioned the empowerment of a vast apparatus of "homeland security" that treats all Americans as potential enemies—with only a *pretense* of even-handedness. In fact, the sense that enemies among us must be dealt with reinforced our bipartisan ruling class's tendency to regard its own domestic political opponents as another set of persons whose backward ways must be guarded against and reformed. A spiral of strife among Americans resulted. In the light of history and of reason, any other outcome would have been surprising.

After 9/11 our ruling class came together on the proposition that, at home as well as abroad, America is at war against enemies so evil that there must be no limit to fighting them, whose identity we must always seek but can never know; that to focus on, to "profile," the kinds of persons who have committed terrorist acts, is racist and provocative; that any American is as likely as any other to be a terrorist, and hence that all must submit to being sifted, screened, restricted—forever. Childhood in the "land of the free, the home of the brave" must now include learning to spread-eagle and be still as government employees run their hands over you. Patriotism is now supposed to mean obeisance to the security establishment, accepting that the authorities may impose martial law on whole cities, keep track of all phone calls, or take whatever action they choose against any person for the sake of "homeland security," and that theirs alone is the choice whether to disclose the basis for whatever they do.

While the Obama administration ceased to use its predecessor's term "war on terror" to describe its actions abroad, it redoubled commitment to "homeland security," reorienting it to home-grown "extremism" defined ad hoc. The result seems less compatible with words such as "peace," than with "Oceania," the country in which George Orwell's novel, *1984,* is set.

Homeland Security as Domestic Nation-Building

George Washington had warned that foreign war naturally increases partisan strife at home. Indeed, strife at home and abroad often stems from the same presumptions of primacy. Recall that during the first half of the nineteenth century, Americans in the North and South devolved into nations yearning to force one another to recognize the superiority of their ways. The resulting Civil War's winners first gloried in their disastrous attempt to reconstruct the losers and then fancied themselves entitled to improve, to reconstruct, lesser beings throughout the world including in the Northern states.

President Woodrow Wilson's personal commitment to forcible reform dated to his post-Civil War student days: "I remember a classmate of mine saying, 'Why, man, can't you let anything alone?' I said, 'I let everything alone that you can show me is not itself moving in the wrong direction, but I am not going to let those things alone that I see going downhill.'"

The point is that, so long and insofar as any ruling class is possessed of this Wilsonian sense of intellectual-moral-political entitlement to nation-build, it must be a disturber of the peace—especially where it has the greatest power to do it. At home.

Instantly after 9/11, our ruling class intoned as a mantra that the event had "changed everything"—in America. But what, why, and to what end? We will now discuss how, post-9/11, our bipartisan ruling class brought home its oblivion of peace, and how this corrodes America's core: the equality and interchangeability of rulers and ruled, liberty, the rule of law, peace among fellow citizens.

Nations, like armies, are seldom as cohesive, so at peace internally, as when *first* confronted by enemies-in-arms. Foreign terrorists having broken America's domestic peace for foreign causes, Americans naturally drew closer to one another against the powers that embody those causes—the several Palestinian powers, Syria, Iraq, Saudi Arabia, Iran, etc.—as well as against their sympathizers and their cultures. But then our ruling class demanded that Americans put out of their minds that 9/11 had been perpetrated by Muslims acting on behalf of Muslim causes; it demanded that the American people put aside the distinction between fellow citizens and those who despise us, between our culture and theirs; that, as a gesture of peace toward the Muslim world, Americans make no distinction between themselves and the people, culture, and causes responsible for 9/11 and nearly all other acts of terror.

That meant demanding that Americans believe that any among ourselves are as likely as not to be terrorists. In sum, it *demanded that Americans trust each other less than ever, but that they trust the authorities more than ever.* Thus having diminished the natural distinctions between citizen and foreigner, familiar and alien, friend and enemy, our ruling class accentuated the artificial distinction between rulers and ruled. The former set of distinctions tends to bind a people together. The latter divides them.

Nevertheless, after a decade of "homeland security," divided as the American people are among themselves, they seem increasingly united in distrusting the US government. Polls taken by the *Washington Post* as well as by *Fox News* after the April 15, 2013, bombing of the Boston Marathon that left 3 people dead and 208 injured, asking whether you fear more "that the government will not go far enough to investigate terrorism . . . or whether it will go too far," found that respondents feared the government more than the terrorists by margins of seven to thirteen points, respectively. By contrast, similar polls after 9/11 had shown a huge reservoir of trust for the government. How did the government waste that trust?

Security as Sovereign

The US Department of Homeland Security's statement of its mission, signed by President George W. Bush, states that: "The terrorist threat to America is an unavoidable byproduct of the technological, educational, economic, and social progress . . . an inescapable reality of life in the 21st century. It is a permanent condition to which America and the entire world must adjust. The need for homeland security, therefore, is not tied to any specific terrorist threat." Any notion that we may rid ourselves of it is unrealistic, because terrorism "takes many forms . . . is often invisible." Because we can never know our enemies, "[w]e can never be sure that we have defeated all of our terrorist enemies."

The homeland-security regime thus established is not limited in focus or scope. Its political substance is to subordinate the people's right to "life, liberty and the pursuit of happiness" under the "laws of Nature and Nature's God"—to the principle that we must live as the security establishment thinks best. The document does not attempt to argue any of the above by appealing to reason through "proposition, objection, and rebuttal." Nor did the Bush administration state the authority by which it imposed what amounts to a constitutional change. Nor were the provisions of the new way of life submitted to any sort of ratification. Rather, homeland security imposes itself through statute read by few and ratified by no one, as well as by the ruling class's inertial force.

Insecuring America

The government's new emphasis on security put additional strain on domestic peace and safety, already under pressure from other causes. Anyone may compare how much more menacing America feels in the twenty-first century from the way it felt as recently as the 1990s: ritual humiliations at the airport, Washington, DC, and government buildings turned into fortresses. Increasingly, airport-style "security" impeding access to major events from sports to wherever VIPs are present. VIPs with bodyguards, as in the third world everywhere demands for identification. Security cameras everywhere.

It takes special effort (and a certain age) to remember life before 1972, when there were no fences around airports, when anyone could walk into any public space unquestioned, and people did not walk around with (easily counterfeited) badges around their necks, when there were not thousands of government employees trained to shepherd us like sheep and we were not expected to act like sheep.

Whereas in 1963 Alabama Sheriff Bull Connor's use of a mere cattle prod to disperse a crowd scandalized the nation, a generation later the police's use of electroshock "tasers" and pepper spray to convulse (and occasionally kill) individuals who talk back to them had become unremarkable, routine, quotidian.

The culture of homeland security is corrosive of freedom. The nightly news inured a generation of Americans to squads of masked-men sporting the words "Police," or "Federal Agent," or "Security" on their backs clattering armored, armed, and menacing into "situations" in time to harass bystanders and hold ritual self-congratulatory press conferences.

The entertainment industry depicts as normal "reality" tales of government agents safeguarding the public by all manner of lawlessness. The 1950s popular TV show *Dragnet* personified that era's peace officers: Its Sergeant Joe Friday wore jacket and tie, rang the doorbell, and addressed citizens with "yes ma'm, no ma'm." But the turn-of-our-century paramilitary heroes of *Dallas SWAT* shout obscenities as they break down doors, shove, and shoot. In our time, it is not unusual for police to shoot unarmed citizens because "I thought he might have a gun." Houston police killed a double ampu-tee in a wheelchair who was wielding a ballpoint pen. Federal police shot dead a woman guilty of reckless driving between the White House and the Capitol, and a California cop killed a 13-year-old boy for carrying a toy plastic rifle. The popular cable TV series 24 was all about "security" agents torturing suspects. The latest version of the video game "Grand Theft" involves the player in torturing a prisoner. Habit-making fun.

Yet ordinary people have never felt less secure. Whereas few Americans felt the need to carry guns in the 1950s, when policemen were few and wore blue, in our time of pervasive "security" millions of Americans feel insecure enough to go about armed. Despite (or because) of regulations that make gun ownership more difficult, the market for guns and ammunition is overwhelmed. It is a falling barometer of confidence in government.

It makes as little sense to ascribe contemporary America's insecurity to citizens' felt need to provide their own as it does to consider fevers as causes rather than symptoms of infections. In fact, the relationship between true security, true peace, and civilization is as tight today as it was when legend has it that king Minos made it unnecessary for ordinary Greeks to go about armed by ridding the Aegean of pirates. Presumably, Minos did so by distinguishing pirates from non-pirates. But contemporary American "security" does not rid us of today's pirates. Rather, pirates of all kinds now multiply because "security" confuses them with peaceable Americans.

Who Is the Enemy?

Discerning who domestic enemies may be and determining what is to be done about them—deciding about war and peace at home—is identical in principle to deciding it internationally. The new American security state's refusal explicitly to distinguish good citizens from terrorists proceeds from the very same agnostic pretense by which our ruling class refuses to pass explicit judgment on the international causes and cultures in whose quarrels it partakes.

But that pretense of agnosticism shields implicit judgments from scrutiny. The Patriot Act of 2001 penalizes giving aid and comfort to terrorist organizations, while empowering the US government to designate any organization, association, or any individual as being somehow associated with "terrorists"—without having to justify to anyone its designation of "terrorists" or of association therewith. But while those designations are ad hoc, they are not random.

Our ruling class, *as a matter of principle and of habit,* has refused publicly to disclose, never mind to debate and to legislate, by what criteria anyone becomes liable to being designated a terrorist or otherwise an "enemy combatant," and what might be done with, to, or about such persons. It treats these very criteria, *supposing they exist,* as state secrets. In practice, it distinguishes, indicts, convicts, and punishes people and ideas they happen not to like at the time for reasons of their own. It covers its actions by leaks to friendly media from high-level sources followed by orchestrated press campaigns. This is reminiscent of what Orwell described in *1984.*

Discretion vs. Law

By way of example, in 2011 we learned from the *New York Times* of a secret document in which our Justice Department describes a set of decisions made during the summer of 2010 ordering and purporting to authorize the nonjudicial killing of a US citizen named Anwar al-Awlaki, the reasoning concerning which, the document takes pains to assure us, would not apply to any other citizen. But, strictly from the *Times'* report, it seems impossible to discern any reason why the document's death sentence would not apply to anyone to whom the president and his advisers might choose to apply it. Here is the *Times'* paraphrase of it:[1]

> The Office of Legal Counsel . . . may have given oral approval for an attack on Mr. Awlaki before completing its detailed memorandum. . . . Mr. Awlaki had been placed on a kill-or-capture list around the time of the attempted bombing of a Detroit-bound airliner on Dec. 25, 2009. Mr. Awlaki was accused of helping to recruit the attacker for that operation. . . . Mr. Awlaki, who was born in New Mexico, was also accused of playing a role in a failed plot to bomb two cargo planes last year, part of a pattern of activities that counterterrorism officials have said showed that he had evolved from merely being a propagandist . . . to playing an operational role in Al Qaeda in the Arabian Peninsula's continuing efforts to carry out terrorist attacks . . . . Based on those premises, the Justice Department concluded that Mr. Awlaki was covered by the authorization to use military force against Al Qaeda that Congress enacted shortly after the terrorist attacks of Sept. 11, . . .

Note that the anonymous accusation itself, not any substantiation thereof, was sufficient for the death sentence, and that the alleged acts of war, "*helping to recruit,*" "*playing a role,*" and "*pattern of activities,*" are subjective judgments, empty of objective meaning about what Awlaki actually did.

The unnamed "counterterrorism officials" took on the power effectively to decide that a state of war exists between the United States and a particular American citizen—*effectively to declare war on an individual American, and to do so secretly.* Moreover, no one seriously contends that any legislator who voted for the congressional authorization that is taken as tantamount to such a declaration of war meant to authorize the nonjudicial killing of an American citizen who is not "in arms," but who is said by *unnamed persons* to have played an *undefined role* in an *undefined organization*'s anti-American activities.

The bureaucrats then make short work of the law: A federal statute that prohibits Americans from murdering other Americans abroad, the officials wrote, did not apply either, because it is not "murder" to kill a wartime enemy in compliance with the laws of war. . . . Then there was the Bill of Rights: the Fourth Amendment's guarantee that a "person" cannot be seized by the government unreasonably, and the Fifth Amendment's guarantee that the government may not deprive a person of life "without due process of law." The memo dealt with that by stating that what is reasonable, and the process that is due, was different for Awlaki than for an ordinary criminal. It cited court cases allowing American citizens who had joined an enemy's forces to be detained or prosecuted in a military court just like noncitizen enemies. But how had Awlaki "joined"? And joined precisely what? No answer.

The unnamed officials set aside the executive order and the statute just by *deeming* that the US citizen to be killed is an enemy in war. But under the US Constitution, the law of war comes into force only when a lawful state of war exists—and only a congressional declaration can create that state. Even if such a state existed, by what criteria had anyone determined that Awlaki was such a combatant? He did not make himself into a combatant self-evidently by appearing "in arms." Nevertheless, say the officials, Awlaki was an imminent risk to innocent people: "The document's authors argued that 'imminent' risks could include those by an enemy leader who is in the business of attacking the United States whenever possible, even if he is not in the midst of launching an attack at the precise moment he is located." But the meaning of "imminent" according to the US government does not correspond to that found in dictionaries of the English language. Rather, the US government decrees that "imminent" now means being involved, in some undefined way, in "*business*" anonymously said to be "bad."

Then in 2013 the Justice Department released an undated, *unsigned* "White Paper"[2] constituting the US government's official position on this matter, confirming the *Times*' account, especially on the key point: an anonymous "high official" of the Justice Department is the ultimate authority over the life and death of an American citizen accused of joining with "al-Qaeda" or an "associate" thereof—whatever those words might mean.

Consider the constitutional reasoning behind this and Section 1021 of the National Defense Authorization Act of 2011. The Bush administration had argued that foreigners who the Executive deem to be "enemies"—unlike American citizens so deemed—are not entitled to constitutional protections arbitrated through legal "due process." Obama, for his part, defended nonjudicial killing of Americans saying: "It's not a bunch of folks in a room somewhere just making decisions. It's part and parcel of our overall authority when it comes to battling al-Qaeda . . . focused at people who are on a list of active terrorists."

Yet his administration's criteria for who is to be killed, and the evidence for each case, are indeed the exclusive purview of "a bunch of folks in a room." How does anyone know that these folks know what they are doing? That their criteria and information make sense? Thus far, the Bush and Obama positions are identical.

But the Obama administration went on to assert that foreigners, like Americans, *are* entitled to some unspecified "due process." But then it defined *this "due process" as something that could take place entirely within the executive branch*. By this assertion the Obama administration, instead of raising foreigners to the legal status of citizens and that of combatants to the status of civilians, downgraded citizens to the status of foreigners and that of civilians to that of combatants. That assertion serves to pre-empt real "due process."

As a result, the president and his advisers constituted themselves at once setters of criteria for enmity, accusers, judges, and killers of whomever they choose.

When the line between war and peace is erased; when the definition of enemies is anybody's guess but in practice is the prerogative of a "high official"; when "battlefield" is defined as the world itself and "arms" are construed to mean words as well as swords; the "decider" may deem anyone to be an enemy-in-arms for whatever reason pleases the "decider." Within which constitution does this fit?

The 2013 memo claims to draw its authority from "the inherent right of the United States to national self-defense under international law . . . and the existence of an armed conflict with al-Qa'ida under international law." Nonsense: No treaty (including adherence to the UN charter's Article 51) *confers* a right to self-defense. Nature itself does that. No treaty authorizes preclusive attack. Nor could any do so. The US armed forces carried out the operations that followed the 9/11 attacks under the US Congress's Authorization for the Use of Military Force (AUMF) of September 2001. But that authority is limited to pursuing people somehow connected to those attacks. Yet the 2013 memo purports to invest the US government with the authority to kill people, including Americans, without even alleging connection with those attacks.

In sum, under Republican and Democratic administrations alike, the US government has been ready, willing, and able to assert authority to treat anyone it chooses, including fellow Americans, as enemies at its discretion.

Berkeley law professor John Yoo spelled out the principle that the law of war justifies its own discretion. Yoo wrote: "The days . . . when our forces against terrorism were limited to the Federal Bureau of Investigation, federal prosecutors, and the criminal justice system will not return." They will not, he wrote, because a four-judge plurality of the Supreme Court agreed that Congress's authorization of "all necessary and appropriate force" against all who may have been involved in the 9/11 attacks instituted a state of war that, he argued, means that henceforth, *implicitly forever,* the president could imprison as a prisoner of war anyone he deems an "enemy combatant" in the exercise of his war power, without justifying it to anybody.

Yoo argued against any limits on such detention: "[While the Court] acknowledged the 'unconventional nature' of the war on terrorism and suggested that if hostilities continued 'for two generations,' [Yaser] Hamdi's detention might indeed exceed the government's war powers . . . the court did not provide any reason why after two generations it may be necessary to reconsider the laws of war. If American troops remain engaged in combat in Afghanistan in 2040, the laws of war do not require the United States to release

Hamdi or other Taliban detainees."[3] Or anybody else for that matter, or to justify it to anyone.

Yoo's argument—the Bush administration's argument, which some Republicans adopted as a badge of partisan pride—is that, war having been more or less authorized at one point but never defined, the US government may do thereafter in the name of war anything it thinks proper, indefinitely—and that it need not bother defining or reconciling its ends and means. Thus a slice of the conservative side of American public life, until recently the defender of individual rights as well as the advocate of winning wars, was led to espouse perpetual executive prerogative in the name of "security."

Note well that this treatment of war, shared by both parties, excludes victory and peace while assuming that endless war *cum* homeland security is sustainable, indefinitely.

Cui Bono?

The least of reasons why it is not is that, in wartime more than ever, government power over domestic life tends to grow beyond the capacity of human beings to use it in nondestructive ways.

If victory and peace—ends that are quintessentially in the interest of the entire body politic—are not the natural end of the discretionary power inherent in war, what is? To whose end will the government exercise its ever-increasing capacity to intrude? Alas, the practical answer is "the discretion of the ruling class, ad hoc, in the interest of the ruling class."

The case of Anwar Awlaki illustrates how the claim of "security" often hides government's garden-variety tendency to cover its own incompetence, or worse. Awlaki's involvement with terrorism predated by almost a decade the events cited in Justice Department memo that sentenced him to death, and his relationship with the US government was something that many in the government have an interest in burying.

According to Congress' still classified "Joint Inquiry Into Intelligence Community Activities Before and After the Terrorist Attacks of September 11, 2001" Awlaki who worked as an Imam at a Saudi-financed mosque in southern California, helped Saudi intelligence officer Osama Bassnan establish two of the 9/11 hijackers on their

arrival in America in 2000. The following year, having been transferred to another Saudi mosque near the Pentagon, he helped the two
to get the IDs with which they boarded the planes that they helped
to hijack. At the time, Awlaki lectured for a foundation financed by
Saudi ambassador Prince Bandar, whose largess had made him everyone's friend in Washington. Deputy Secretary of Defense Gordon
England had Awlaki talk to the top Pentagon executives about how
to get along with Muslims. In 2002, though, US customs arrested
Awlaki, but released him to a "Saudi representative on orders of the
FBI." He later fled the US on a Saudi aircraft.

Just before 9/11, Mohammed Atta, the hijackers' leader, visited the
Sarasota, Florida home of Esam Ghazzawi, an adviser to the Saudi
royal family. The day before the attack, Saudi official Saleh Hussayen
stayed in the same Marriot at Dulles airport as three of the hijackers.
Two days after the attacks, President George W. Bush received Prince
Bandar at the White House, accepted his assurances, and evacuated
from the US an unspecified number of Saudi officials, plus the family
of Osama bin Laden. Since that time, the US government has done its
best to quash inquiries into the role of Saudis in 9/11.

Concern for the safety of good Americans might just possibly not
have been as powerful a motivator for killing Awlaki as solicitude
for the reputations of not-so-competent or not-so-honest US government officials.

Well before 9/11, we had foretastes of what discretionary police
powers mean in practice. Consider the modern security state's legal
paradigm: the Racketeer Influenced and Corrupt Organizations
(RICO) Act of 1970. Passed to facilitate conviction of persons *somehow* connected with the Mafia—guys with names like Rico—since the
1990s RICO has been used against political enemies of every administration in power, most recently against pro-life organizations.

The "Iron Law"

The point is that the lack of explicit standards on which society
has deliberated and agreed—*that is, of law specified clearly and
enforced impartially*—invites those in power to make up standards,
specs, policies, and rules as they go along, for their own convenience.
Those in power become the law.

Inevitably, following the path of least resistance and maximum political advantage, the extension of post-9/11 police power in the name of fighting terrorism ended up serving partisan ends and degrading our peace.

The attempt to establish security without identifying, much less eliminating, those responsible for insecurity has transformed American life. *Apolitical policing of public life starts as impotent, random harassment.* It ends, as Machiavelli wrote, in the empowerment of those who command the government to police for their own ends, and in the majority's increasing alienation from the regime.

That is because it is impossible for officials who make up standards implicitly and unaccountably to do so apolitically. It would be strange indeed were decisions about the public's enemies to abstract from the private prejudices and interests, from the partisan friendships and enmities of the human beings who make them. James Madison (*Federalist #51*) wrote that the American regime is based on the explicit recognition of interests and biases. Neglecting that, and barring explicit political decisions from the front door, ensures that implicit political decisions flood in through the windows.

The point here is that our ruling class's judgments about friends and enemies are not based on defensible criteria. *If such criteria existed, they would be the very same thing as "profiles" that screen bad guys from good, the very same thing as standards for security clearances.* Such criteria would be set transparently, and those who set them could be held responsible for their substance. But, since the early 1970s, investigators for clearances have been ordered not to ask for or listen to, much less consider, any information about a person's religion or politics.

Hence, the badge around the neck of the FBI agent or of the guy in the nuclear power plant's control room is no more assurance that he will not commit mayhem than were the clearances granted to US Army Major Nidal Hassan, who killed thirteen fellow soldiers and wounded twenty-nine at Fort Hood, Texas. His business card—an advertisement rather than a secret—identified him as a "Soldier of Allah." You should not imagine that the US government's criteria for access to America's most sensitive positions are qualitatively different from the ones by which it cleared Hassan.

Inevitably, then, apolitical policing is a pretense. By 2012, a Rasmussen poll showed that 64 percent of Americans were more afraid of terrorist attack from other Americans than from foreigners. No surprise. That had been the ruling class's message for a decade. The focus on "homeland security" had succeeded in adding the suspicion of terrorism on top of all the reasons that Americans had to distrust and to blame one another for their troubles. But of whom should we be afraid?

Should the American people worry about, surveil, discourage, restrict, Muslims—visitors or home grown—who might have taken up jihad? The ruling class says, No, look elsewhere: Republican President George W. Bush reacted to 9/11, and Democratic President Barack Obama and Army Chief of Staff General George Casey reacted to Major Hassan's 2010 murder of fellow soldiers at Fort Hood, Texas, and to the 2013 Boston Marathon bombing, by adjuring the American people not to attribute the carnage to any particular set of people, that is, to Islamists. On whom, then should "security" focus? By branding the obvious as politically incorrect, the ruling class made the designation "dangerous extremists" a matter of subjective likes and dislikes. But whose likes and dislikes?

Naturally, persons who possess the greatest power in government and society have the larger opportunity to direct blame and distrust, even to direct mayhem, onto those they like least. Since the mid-1990s, authoritative voices from Democratic President Bill Clinton to Republican New York Mayor Michael Bloomberg, echoed by the media, have intoned a familiar litany: America is beset by violence from racism, sexism, homophobia, and religious obscurantism, by domestic abuse, greed, and gun owners. These ills are not so different from those found in backward parts of the world where we fight "extremism" in order to fight terrorism. Indeed, these ills argue for fighting extremism, indeed for nation-building in America as well as abroad.

Whose Enemy?

Who in America embodies extremism? Who is inherently responsible for social ills, including terrorism? Who will have to be "nation-built," reconstructed? What kind of people will have to have a new and better way of life forced upon them? No surprise: The ruling class's political opponents, the conservative side of American life.

This started long ago. In 1963, the notion that President John F. Kennedy's assassination was due to the "climate of hatred" in conservative Dallas, Texas, was rife in the ruling class, even though the assassin, Lee Harvey Oswald, was a Communist who had spent two years in the Soviet Union working with its GRU military intelligence service. The narrative is consistent. On the fiftieth anniversary of Kennedy's assassination, the NBC network aired a show that continued the narrative of Dallas, the conservative killer city, without mentioning that the assassin was a Communist.

Today, computer searches find that the term "extremist" correlates in the major newspapers with "conservative" or "right wing" at twelve times the rate it does with "liberal" or "left wing." Mayor Michael Bloomberg encapsulated the normalcy of this conflation when he imputed an attempted bombing of Times Square (by a jihadist, as it turned out) to "someone with a political agenda that doesn't like the health care bill or something."

No surprise, also, that, since 2006, the Department of Homeland Security has used its intelligence "fusion centers" to compile ominously worded dossiers against such groups as "pro-lifers" and such "antigovernment activists" as "homeschoolers" and "gun owners." DHS has its own police force, the Federal Protective Service, that conducts monitoring and harassment of such groups, and conducts its "practice runs" against mockups of these groups. The FBI for its part infiltrates the Tea Parties as it once did the Communist Party—agent of the Soviet Union that it was.

This choice of targets follows not from any policy but from a view of America that is part of the ruing class's identity. In January 2012, the DHS, in cooperation with the University of Maryland, published a study entitled *Hot Spots of Terrorism and Other Crimes in the United States, 1979–2008*. It classified as "extreme right wing terrorists" persons whom it judges to be "suspicious of centralized federal authority" or "reverent of individual liberty." In July 2012, Colonel Kevin Benson of the US Army's University of Foreign Military and Cultural Studies at Fort Leavenworth, Kansas, and Jennifer Weber of the University of Kansas published an article in the *Small Wars*

Journal titled "Full Spectrum Operations in the Homeland: A 'Vision' of the Future," arguing that the US Army should prepare itself for contingencies such as "extremist militia motivated by the goals of the 'tea party' movement" seizing a small town. The article argues that the Army's Operating Concept 2016–2028 obliges "the military to execute without pause and as professionally as if it were acting overseas." In 2013, the US Military Academy's Combating Terrorism Center published a paper that cited approvingly the Southern Poverty Law Center's (SPLC) indictment of the "far right"—which it defined as "conservatives"—as threats to national security. The SPLC is also a regular collaborator of the Department of Homeland Security. No official act is needed for likeminded persons at the top of society to act in mutually pleasing ways.

Nor, between 2001 and 2010, was any official act needed for the FBI to confine its vast, fruitless effort to find the source of weapons-grade anthrax in the postal system to a hypothetical American (white) "mad, right-wing scientist"—an effort that drove one person to suicide and another to win a $5.6 million lawsuit against the US government for harassment, *but that charged no one with anything.*

Nor was it cause for wonder when, in 2010–2012, the Internal Revenue Service audited over 500 conservative organizations concerned with "government spending, government debt or taxes; education of the public by advocacy/lobbying to make America a better place to live; statements in the case file criticize how the country is being run." The IRS included Catholic and evangelical organizations, as well as the Tea Parties, demanding that its targets reveal details about their donors, whom it then audited aggressively along with donors to conservative candidates for office. In some cases, the IRS turned over these donor lists to the conservative organizations' opponents for further harassment. One conservative who had formed a voter registration group had her business audited not just by the IRS, but by the FBI's domestic terrorism unit, the Bureau of Alcohol, Tobacco, and Firearms, the Environmental Protection Agency, and the Occupational Safety and Health Administration (OSHA), as well. Moreover, when the targeted groups protested peacefully at IRS headquarters, they were met by armed DHS guards and helicopters, as befits presumed terrorists who are to be guarded against.

None of this is law, or even official policy, much less conspiracy. Rather, it reflects the prejudices and convenience, the intellectual, social, indeed the very *identity* of those in power. After all, in September 2010, President Barack Obama had called "enemies of democracy" the very groups that the IRS then subjected to punitive audits, and Vice President Joseph Biden had called some of them "terrorists." In September and October 2013, in the context of a controversy over congressional appropriations, Obama administration spokesmen referred to these very same groups as "terrorists," "jihadists," "hostage takers," etc. Indeed, a Rasmussen poll showed that 26 percent of the Obama administration's supporters—possibly not the least influential among them—*regard the Tea Parties as the top terrorist threat to America*. Democratic senators and self-proclaimed "good government" groups aligned with them had written to the IRS urging the audits. So had President Obama's White House counsel before taking office. Authoritatively, the IRS commissioners' wife headed one of the groups clamoring for the audits.

Why should not officials all across the US government—from the IRS to the EPA to the Federal Elections Commission—act according to their superiors' opinions, to what they hear from the best people and what they read in the best media, indeed according to their shared beliefs? Do not society's most authoritative voices bolster those beliefs by indicting the conservative side of American life as extremists? Do not significant sectors of society applaud actions against them?

If such Americans really were "enemies of democracy," if the Tea Parties terrorized the land, if the Catholic Church and evangelical organizations indeed were waging a "war on women," if the Family Research Council were as "hateful and "bigoted" as the DHS's Southern Poverty Law Center claims, if these American conservatives were truly the American version of the Taliban, then why should a government at war with extremism not save itself and society's best elements from them? Why should it not use its official and officious powers to discourage, discredit, diminish them, make life difficult for them, make war on them insofar as possible? Why should it not help the party of good government and of good people prevail in a close election?

The Spiral of Strife

Whereas, in 1861, Lincoln had sought to head off civil war by forswearing discrimination against his opponents, our current ruling class builds support for itself among its constituencies precisely by such discrimination.

Alas, Newton's Third Law applies to politics in our time as much as it ever did. Why should those targeted not return the favor with compound interest? Which party first deprives its opponents of peace and starts the spiral of strife is irrelevant. *All human beings naturally crave excuses for treating their political opponents as bad people, as public enemies.* As Thucydides's account of Corcyra reminds us, using government power to hurt political opponents draws all into a spiral increasingly destructive of all. As more and more Americans succumb to this temptation, domestic peace slips away. Homeland Security has helped lead America into that spiral, the exit from which is harder than the entry.

The problem is not "profiling." It is profiling of the *implicit, irresponsible* kind that happens to be wrong. Lack of accountability and transparency in decisions about friends and enemies means free rein for bureaucracies and ruling classes to justify their prejudices and to cover their insufficiencies.

If war, once exceptional, is henceforth normal and perpetual, and if all are liable to be treated as enemies, our complex of laws boils down to the Roman dictatorial formula: *salus populi suprema lex.* In the name of the people's safety, the dictator's will is law. But republican Rome's "dictators" were appointed for brief emergencies for the purpose of returning the state to its ordinary laws, and themselves to live under them. Not incidentally, they were congenitally committed to victory. By contrast, the new American security state is committed neither to victory, nor to any purpose that transcends it. Least of all is it committed to transcending itself. Like Orwell's Oceania, it is an endless end in itself.

The difference between America and Oceania, however, is all-important. Oceania's subjects were Europeans, who suffered their rulers' miserable wisdom without question. Americans don't do that.

22

What Can Be America's Peace?

Our ruling class seems united in refusing to think seriously about peace. President Obama, conscious that Americans are averse to permanent war, solemnly declared: "This war, like all other wars, must end."[1] He recalled James Madison's warning that "no nation could preserve its freedom in the midst of continual warfare." He said, moreover, that it is not good to grant presidents "unbound powers more suited for traditional armed conflicts." But, having bowed to generalities, Obama did not indicate how this war might be brought to an end. Rather, he proposed to enshrine in law the practice of designating persons, including Americans, as enemies without a constitutional declaration of war—and killing them.

The *Wall Street Journal*'s editorial page confirmed the ruling class's unity with a reply less artful but more honest: dismissing "the understandable American yearning for peace" as a child's immature cravings, it concluded that there should be more killing at executive discretion rather than less. It went on to state that "the US has done very well balancing security and freedom since 9/11," as well as that the War on Terror's "struggle in the shadows" and its cosmetic consequences should be accepted as indefinite.[2]

Unsustainable

Yet the modern American status of no peace, no war is unsustainable internationally and domestically. Internationally, the logic of commitments without end drains America's spirit and makes us contemptible to foreigners. The expenditure of thousands of lives and trillions of dollars in the Middle East diminished America's capacity to weigh on events everywhere and convinced a generation of humanity that we can be had. Republican George W. Bush and Democrat Barack Obama vied to persuade the Muslim world how much they respect Islam. Both reaped worse disrespect for America, swallowed it, and made it worse. Vladimir Putin's Russia treats America with contempt. In East Asia, the US government's continued diminution of military power, as well as repeated deference to Chinese requests to absorb North Korea's repeated violations of agreements, made America less relevant. From Britain to Benghazi, US diplomatic representatives have reason to fear for their lives. Americans who have dual passports increasingly travel under their other identity. It's safer. As the years pass, Americans sense ever less respect from abroad, and more cause to fear.

At home the American people grow more skeptical about the post-9/11 security state despite the scarcity of leaders who champion their sentiments. Americans reacted to the 2013 revelation that the National Security Agency (NSA) has access to every unencrypted computer message, and that it is recording the instance (and in the case of cellphones, the location) of every call in America with disbelief in the excuse that this protects us from terrorists. Correctly so. NSA director General Keith B. Alexander was forced to admit to the Senate Judiciary Committee that his previous claim that its surveillance had prevented fifty-four terrorist attacks was false. The real figure was "maybe one or two."[3]

Americans know that blanket, unfocused electronic surveillance did not prevent the 2013 bombing of the Boston Marathon. Persons intent on hiding electronic communications from the NSA can do so either by purchasing bank-grade encryption systems or, cheaply, by using prepaid cellphones or computer accounts on a one-time basis. Ordinary caution works well too. Every new terrorist event reminds Americans of homeland security's impotence. Yet Americans also sense that unfocused homeland security offers the government's many agencies the opportunity to focus their attention on anyone suspected of violating their countless regulations and policies.

The American people increasingly see their ruling class as inept, burdensome, and harbingers of trouble. Public opinion polls show that only about one in seven Americans is confident that his children will live as well as the present generation, and that only 18 percent trust the federal government to "do the right thing most of the time." The part of the ruling class that deals with national security is catching up with the levels of popular rejection already experienced by the rest. Its political correctness grates. Its partisan presumption of moral authority to nation-build American society as it does foreign ones guarantees partisan warfare.

Forgotten Fundamentals

Whatever unease with accepting endless strife as the new normal may exist within the establishment, it has not reached the fruitful point of asking: Just why is peace impossible? Does anything written in the stars condemn America to being a garrison state at war with itself? If not, where did *we* go wrong? What have *we* forgotten?

Simply, our ruling class has forgotten who Americans are and what way of life is proper to America, as well as the basic rules of international affairs. The search for peace would have to begin with rethinking the fundamentals: What is to be America's peace and, given our current situation, how might we get it?

The pursuit of peace was central to American statecraft until the twentieth century because American statesmen prized America's unique identity and, hence, the life that could be lived only in America, only in peace. They prized peace to make sure that the growing nation's engagement with the world would not interfere with life at home. They regarded war as a means to secure America's peace. Commitment to peace lapsed among American statesmen as they confused America's unique civilization with their own preferences, aimed to impose these preferences on mankind, and blurred the line between war and peace. This made for perpetual war with foreigners and for increased strife among Americans.

[margin note: American exceptionalism]

Henceforth, to live in peace among ourselves and among nations, Americans need statesmen newly committed to the civilization that had made America unique. Breaking the past century's dysfunctional habits, they would recover our founders' priorities and practices.

That would require intellectual understanding, moral resolve, and political skill. This book can contribute only understanding.

New Statesmanship

America needs a new generation of statesmen, who regard minding America's business—acting as the American people's fiduciary agents, *minding America's peace and winning America's wars*—not as a demotion but as a calling that absorbs the highest human talents and confers the highest honors. They would cast aside pretenses of shaping mankind, remembering that to the extent that America has improved the rest of the world, it has done so by being different in an exemplary manner. They would regain appreciation that America's cultural-political identity is immensely worthy, and, hence, that shielding America's domestic peace from foreign influence is itself their proper goal.

America's paramount interest is remaining itself, remaining the place to which would-be Americans born elsewhere come to live in a unique way, without a ruling class. Along with Lincoln, we cannot stress enough that dedication to the proposition that "all men are created equal" is the heart and soul of what makes America different from the rest of the world. Preserving that exceptional nature is American statecraft's natural, paramount objective.

Twenty-first-century Americans want neither more, nor less, from foreign nations than did Americans in Washington's or Adams's time: peaceful, reciprocal respect. But, whereas two centuries ago foreigners stinted respect to an America too weak to command it, in our time they deny it to an America whose wealth they envy, whose pretenses they resent, whose power they no longer fear, and which they no longer trust to fulfill their hopes.

Whether it is possible or not for twenty-first-century America to transcend accumulated resentments, returning America to international relations based on arms-length reciprocal respect would require statesmen to be mindful of Pericles's warning to war-weary Athenians against dreaming that they could just turn their backs on the foreign policy they had followed for a generation. Nevertheless, gradual and sinuous as wise changes in US foreign policy would have to be, the intellectual changes would have to begin simply with reversing the Progressive movement's erasure of the distinction between America's interest and that of mankind, between what is "our business" and what is "their business," between peace and war.

Distinctions

unilaterlism

Then our statesmen would have to affirm their craft's forgotten fundamental: *that the search for peace begins with neutrality in others' affairs and that when others trouble our peace we impose it upon them by war—war as terribly decisive as we can make it.*

George Washington admonished Americans to observe "good faith and justice toward all nations," fully conscious that many of these were enemies and that all were unalterably alien. To Washington, how these quarreled at home and abroad mattered only insofar as they affected America. Washington taught that maintaining America's uniqueness requires keeping the rest of the world at arms' length politically and psychologically. That means that, while the United States' interests will concur with others' from time to time, the concurrence will always be contingent and coincidental, as John Quincy Adams explained to the Monroe cabinet in 1823.

Thus, also, Dwight Eisenhower dedicated much of his presidency to building a military posture that would allow the United States to deal with threats to its own peace definitively, with as little mobilization of civilian society as possible.

In Washington and Adams's time, as in our own, some foreign nations were undergoing revolutions while others were taking sides therein. The founders' advice about such things is worth heeding today: Americans cannot resolve such quarrels. Trying to do that enmeshes us in others' priorities, in ways of thinking and doing that draw us away from our proper agenda, from our priority in remaining American. Peaceably resolving domestic quarrels about what it means to be American is divisive enough without our complicating it with foreign considerations.

The distinction between "our business" and "their business" is the ultimate foundation of peace—the natural limiting principle of international affairs (as it is of interpersonal affairs). American foreign policy, as conceived by Washington and explained by Adams, was based on this distinction, on this "golden rule" of mutual forbearance. America would mind only its own business, fight only its own battles, not because it was weak, but because others' business is their own just as much as ours is our own, because no one has constituted Americans as judges of others' business, and because, while others may forbear much that we might do in our own interest, they will not stand for anything we might presume to do in theirs.

A modern statesmanship of peace, channeling Washington and Adams, would renounce any *substantive* interest in foreign lands, interesting itself only in what affects our own peace and prosperity. This is no more the counsel of retreat than was that of Washington, Lincoln, or Theodore Roosevelt—men on Mt. Rushmore.

Besides, "our business" is all that we may hope actually to affect in lands ruled by others. Thus Theodore Roosevelt worried that his note to Russia's tsar on behalf of the victims of the 1905 pogroms might worsen the Jews' fate. Questions of right aside, involvement in others' business without dominating them is the very definition of irresponsibility.

Our Business

What is "our business"?

Our military defense is very much our business, because, as always, our peace, like anyone's, depends on the power to defend it. But what peace is it that we shall prepare to defend? Means must match ends. Defending global presence *cum* intrusion into others' business is as impossible practically as it is morally indefensible. Consider, for example, the threat posed by nuclear-armed ballistic missiles. Much as Americans would prefer that few peoples—or none—build and possess such things, it is undeniable that any government that wants them can have them, and that the only means of making sure that a people that wants them shall not have them is to occupy such people forcibly and permanently—to make *all* of their business our business.

Since this cannot happen, there is no reasonable alternative to building the best missile defenses that we can (along with the rest of a respectable military establishment) and, behind that shield, to wield diplomacy and military power to guard our peace and win our wars.

Guarding the peace means securing other nations' respect, because respect is as indispensable to peace as its opposite, contempt, is the oxygen of war.

Earning respect and guarding respect is our most immediate duty to peace. That requires guarding against what John Jay called the "just" and "unjust" causes of war (*Federalist* #3 and #4). Now, as then, that means giving no offense and suffering none. Careful as we should be lest we offend, even through well-meant gratuitous suggestions about the right way to live—even in response to foreigners' requests—we must keep in mind that what others take as offenses is their business. They will resent what they choose to resent. Any attempt not to offend those who look for offense is vain. But whoever offends us or intrudes on our independence gives us the most just of all causes to reestablish the respect that is due to us. The choice between killing to force respect, and forgetting the standards by which we live, is to be avoided. But if unavoidable, it must be faced squarely.

Respect means a reputation for never leaving a favor unrewarded or an injury or slight unpunished. Nothing is harder to maintain nor easier to lose than such a reputation. Making fearful examples of anyone who disrespects us is the most just of war's causes and also the definitive way of enforcing our peace.

Syria, Islam, China

Consider the Assad family's dictatorship of Syria from the perspective of America's interest in our own peace. That priority should govern the perspective by which American statesmen should have regarded the Assad regime. Based from its inception in 1970 on the minority Alawite sect and the Ba'ath Party, the Assad regime was congenitally brutal to its people. In 2011, Syria's Sunni majority rose in revolt against the regime, which then made war against that majority.

Some Americans argued that the US government should have relieved the Syrian people's suffering by supporting the insurgency, whether by arming some insurgents or by bombing the regime's stores of chemical weapons. This would have made it easier for Syrian insurgents to kill their enemies. But some of these insurgents count among their enemies Syria's circa three million Christians. Many are members of the Muslim brotherhood, or Wahabis, who have taken part in anti-American terrorism. It is not clear by what right or to what good we Americans should foster a set of killings, the bounds of which we know not and cannot control, nor, above all, whom that would benefit. Thus Syria's internal struggle falls under the heading of "their business."

On the other hand, it was always clear that, the Assad regime being congenitally an enemy of America, exterminating as many of its members as possible for their many acts of bloody enmity to America over two generations would have been rightful recompense, and a healthy warning to anyone who might trouble America—"our business."

Again and again, the Assad regime made itself America's business. In 1982, the Assads made war on Israel through the PLO in Lebanon, and were defeated by Israel's alliance with the Lebanese government. After that, as the US government sought to help Lebanon reestablish control over its territory, Syrian agents truck-bombed the US Marine barracks in Beirut, killing 243 of them. Had the US government responded properly to this act of war, the Assads would never have troubled anyone again. Instead, Republican and Democratic administrations eased Syria's control of Lebanon. By 2003, when the United States invaded Iraq, the Assads were waging war on Israel's northern border as Iran's main proxy through the terrorist group Hizbullah. The Assads quickly made Syria into the headquarters of anti-US forces and the main funnel through which suicide bombers, as well as sophisticated weapons, killed Americans. A weapon from Syria accounted for the only US Abrams tank killed in Iraq. At that time, the 150,000 US troops in Iraq were more than enough to inspire and support whom we wished to overthrow the Assads, or simply to overthrow them. Instead, the US government contented itself with impotent requests for good behavior. By 2006, an emboldened Syria had provoked war between Hizbullah and Israel. But, as Israel's military operations were crippling this arm of America's enemies, the US government stopped the Israelis.

In short, the US government has wasted plenty of opportunities to force America's peace. Two perspectives. Two conclusions.

Although the realities of the Syrian civil war of 2011 argued against US interference, they also created new opportunities for advancing our interests. Making sure of Lebanon's independence from Hizbullah, Syria, and Iran while these were otherwise occupied was very much in America's interest. Nevertheless, the Obama administration chose to join with Russia effectively to guarantee the Assad regime's permanence in exchange for an agreement to rid that regime of chemical weapons—an agreement that no one has any intention of enforcing and which is all but theoretically irrelevant to America's peace. Thus did it turn an opportunity to mind America's business into another occasion for disrespecting America.

To what extent and in what way might the rise of popular Islamist movements from the bulge of Africa to the Philippine archipelago be any of our business? President Obama's "Islam has always been a part of America's history" is the reverse of the truth. Until our time, America's main involvement with the Islamic world had been with the Barbary pirates. Our time's main sociopolitical movements in the Muslim world—the Muslim Brotherhood and the secular-socialist Ba'ath—grew in alliance with or were inspired by Nazi Germany. Their avowed primary reason for being is hate of the westernizing regimes that govern the Muslim world. But Western elites—including our statesmen—seem eager to accept whatever blame for the Muslim world's troubles Muslim politicians impute to Western civilization. That eagerness is the source of the Muslim world's increasing disrespect for America and Americans.

Hence, we should not even try to imagine what Islamists might cite to excuse anti-American violence. Rather, we can and must guard against what surely destroys respect: As the US government failed to hold local rulers responsible for their subjects' disrespect of us, that murderous disrespect grew, and involved countless persons theretofore innocent. Our business now is forcefully to restore respect for ourselves by holding those rulers responsible. The longer we wait, the more force will be needed.

What is our business with China—a vital trading partner and a brutal dictatorship that seeks to replace US influence as far eastward into the Pacific Ocean as it can? We can learn from the fact that America's founders also had valuable trade relations with the despotism *par excellence* of the age, namely Russia. John Quincy Adams's diplomacy vis-à-vis Russia suggests how we might distinguish and harmonize America's and China's business in our time.

In Adams's time, Russia had put itself at the head of a "holy alliance" that threatened to extend its sway into the Western Hemisphere. The emperor of Russia had stated forcefully his view that monarchical rule is better than republican government. But he had maintained peaceful trade with America. Adams's diplomacy had three objectives: 1) to strengthen the peace that existed between the two countries; 2) to state that America would oppose any expansion of monarchy in the Western Hemisphere; and 3) to state America's commitment to republicanism at least as strongly as the emperor had touted monarchy.

In our time, it is worthwhile to reaffirm that our business with China is peaceful, mutually advantageous trade. It is also worthwhile to convey to the Chinese that it is our business and ours alone what relationship with the nations of East Asia would best serve our military security, and that we will support our decisions militarily. For the sake of peace, America must never repeat what happened after 1921, when it committed to a presence in, and made treaty commitments about, the Pacific Rim without fortifying the islands thereof. And most of all, it is worthwhile to affirm what we are about. This does not mean now berating the Chinese as Cordell Hull berated the Japanese in the 1930s. It does mean leaving no doubt that we intend to live by the "laws of nature and nature's God"—if indeed we do.

In sum, what any regime does to its own people and with its own resources is its business. But any regime makes itself America's business insofar as it may break America's peace. By that token, the Adams who famously said that America "does not go abroad in search of monsters to destroy" wrote the previously referenced defense of General Andrew Jackson's raid into Spanish territory that shot the terrorists and ceremoniously hanged the leaders from whom the local authorities were unwilling or unable to protect Americans. But, while Adams wished aloud for a navy big enough to exterminate the equally barbaric Barbary pirates, he did not propose trying to do this, because that navy was lacking. Two sets of monsters had made themselves America's business. But in the case of one monster, a highly imperfect peace was preferable to a war that America did not know how to end in a better peace.

Winning the Peace

Whereas once upon a time such reasoning was fundamental for America's statesmen, it is now conventional wisdom that war, victory, and peace are archaic, not to mention vulgar remnants of a less sophisticated age. Herbert Hoover's reticence in 1931 even to call Japan's aggression and treaty-breaking by their name was arguably a bad choice. But it was based on the true fact that calling treaty-breaking by its name would have told Japan "America stands in your way." Hoover did not speak because he was not willing to stand in Japan's way. But neither were Cordell Hull and Franklin Roosevelt willing to stand in Japan's way. Yet they spoke harshly to Japan without economic, diplomatic, or military plans for a peace acceptable to both sides or imposed by one. And the war came.

Discernment of what does and does not impinge on our peace is essential because there is no such thing as a small war any more than a small pregnancy. It was to avoid war that Theodore Roosevelt taught and practiced proportion between the tenor of words and the size of sticks; because, when war comes, when some states begin to kill and others to take sides, the logic of fear and honor, the multiplicity of passions, drive events beyond anyone's control. In 431 BC, when mighty Athens intervened against Corinth on Corcyra's behalf, which had intervened in tiny Epidamnus's internal affairs, it surely did not mean to stake Greek civilization. Nor, in 1861, did either the Union or Confederacy mean to kill two percent of the United States' population. The combatants of 1914 expected to be home for Christmas, with European civilization intact.

Awareness of the stakes, laser-like focus on a vision of the peace that is to follow, green-eye-shade comparison of costs and benefits, are the albeit-imperfect guides for planning the transition from peace to peace.

Anesthetized by concepts such as "engagement," "crisis management," and "exit strategy," American statesmen have put peace out of mind, often through seemingly innocuous political commitments, and especially through commitments that they did not really mean to fulfill, on the assumption that they would not have to fulfill them. Yet making commitments that carry with them the possibility of war implies an "entering strategy," followed by management to a new state of peace — not by helter-skelter scrambling to get through the latest flap.

Strategy had better stress speed, above all, because time increases war's stakes, uncertainty, and damage, especially at home. There is no record of people's mores or institutions improving in wartime. They worsen as the war drags. The worst happens among peoples under siege: As hope for peace vanishes, as people turn on each other, garrison states collapse from within, regardless of the correlation of forces. Hence, when the US government conceived the "war on terror" as permanent, concentrated it on "homeland security," and directed it against all citizens equally rather than on plausible enemies discriminately, it stumbled into a state of domestic siege that foredoomed America to systemic strife.

No act of terrorism has hurt America so much as have the theory and practice of homeland security, and none threaten to undo America's foundations so much as does our ruling class's increasing tendency to deem their domestic opponents "terrorists," and the clear and present prospect of their acting accordingly. Homeland security's pretense of agnosticism as to who America's enemies might be has augmented the ruling class's power. That fueled its sense of moral-political-intellectual entitlement to nation-build fellow Americans, and has given civil strife's deadly spiral its first deadly turns among us. Each turn is less resistible than the previous. *No one has explained why any American should accept to live without the prospect of peace with foreigners and as a suspect in his own land.*

As ever, "peace among ourselves" is more important, more urgent, than is peace "with all nations." As ever, peace on the home front is the sine qua non of earning peace with foreigners. There is no recipe for establishing "peace among ourselves and with all nations." That has to be won and preserved as it ever has been here and elsewhere: by reaffirming our way of life, by making friendship with one another the primordial objective of public life, by avoiding the near occasion of war; but, when war is necessary, by fighting it to victory or to the best peace that honestly acknowledged defeat can manage.

Notes

1. Introduction

1. George Washington, Farewell Address of 1796, Papers of George Washington, University of Virginia, 22–27, http://gwpapers.virginia.edu.

2. John Quincy Adams, Speech on Independence Day, 1821, http://www.teachingamericanhistory.org.

3. Ibid.

4. Theodore Roosevelt, *America and the World War* (New York: Charles Scribner's Sons, 1915), 36.

2. Peace, Civilization, and War

1. Thucydides, *History of the Peloponnesian War*, 2.37–2.40, trans. Richard Crawley, ed. Robert B. Strassler (New York: Free Press, 1996), 112–13.

2. Ibid., 3.82, 199–200.

3. *Defensor Pacis*

1. Inscription quoted in Paolo Diacono, *Storia dei Longobardi*, trans. Antonio Zanella (Biblioteca Universale Rizzoli, 1991), 482.

2. Aurelia Henry, ed. and trans., *The De Monarchia of Dante Alighieri* (Boston and New York: Houghton Mifflin, 1904), bk. 1, ch. 4.

3. Oliver J. Thatcher, ed., *The Library of Original Sources*, vol. 5: *The Early Medieval World* (Milwaukee: University Research Extension, 1907), 423.

4. Patriot Kings

1. Henry St. John, Viscount Bolingbroke, *The Works of Lord Bolingbroke* (Philadelphia: Carey and Hart, 1841), 2:417.

5. A Right to Peace

1. Thomas Jefferson, "A Summary View of the Rights of British America," *The Founders' Constitution,* vol. 1, chap. 14, doc. 10, http://press-pubs.uchicago .edu/founders/documents/v1ch14s10.html.

2. John Allen, "An Oration, upon the Beauties of Liberty" (1773), in *Political Sermons of the American Founding Era, 1730–1805,* ed. Ellis Sandoz (Indianapolis, IN: Liberty Press, 1991), 301.

3. Jefferson, "A Summary View."

6. America, Not Rome

1. Samuel Cooper, "A Sermon Delivered on the Day of the Commencement of the Constitution" (1780), in *Political Sermons of the American Founding Era, 1730–1805,* ed. Ellis Sandoz (Indianapolis, IN: Liberty Press, 1991), 627.

2. Ezra Stiles, "The United States Elevated to Glory and Honor," in *The Pulpit of the American Revolution,* ed. John Wingate Norton, (Boston: Gould and Lincoln, 1860), 397–404.

3. Elhanan Winchester, "A Century Sermon on the Glorious Revolution," in *Political Sermons of the American Founding Era, 1730–1805,* ed. Ellis Sandoz (Indianapolis, IN: Liberty Fund, 1991), 969.

7. Washington's Peace

1. George Washington, "The Farewell Address, 1796," Papers of George Washington, University of Virginia, 22–27, http://gwpapers.virginia.edu.

9. American Geopolitics

1. John Quincy Adams's speech on Independence Day, 1821, http://www .teachingamericanhistory.org.

2. John Quincy Adams to Hugh Nelson, 28 April 1823, in *The Writings of John Quincy Adams,* ed. Worthington C. Ford (New York: Macmillan, 1913–17), 7:369–70.

10. What Greatness?

1. Roy P. Basler, ed., *The Collected Works of Abraham Lincoln* (New Brunswick, NJ: Rutgers University Press, 1953), 1:109.

2. John L. O' Sullivan, "The Great Nation of Futurity," *The United States Democratic Review,* 6, no. 23 (1839).

3. Stephen Douglas at Freeport, in Baster, *The Collected Works,* 3:55.

4. Abraham Lincoln, in Basler, *The Collected Works,* 3:235.

5. Alexander Stephens, of Georgia, on the subject of the Mexican War, delivered in the US House of Representatives, June 16, 1846. Printed by J. and G. S. Gideon, Washington, DC, 1846.

6. Walt Whitman in *The Brooklyn Eagle,* May 11 and June 6, 1846, cited in Archie P. McDonald, ed., *The Mexican War: Crisis for American Democracy* (Lexington, MA: D. C. Heath, 1969), 47–48.

11. Lincoln's Peace

1. Basler, *The Collected Works of Abraham Lincoln* (1953), 4:269.
2. Ibid., 439.
3. Worthington Chauncey Ford and Charles Francis Adams, *John Quincy Adams: His Connection with the Monroe Doctrine and with Emancipation under Martial Law* (Cambridge, MA: John Wilson and Sons, 1902), 75.

12. Peacefully Pregnant

1. Walter McDougall, *Promised Land, Crusader State: The American Encounter with the World since 1776* (Boston: Houghton Mifflin, 1999), 109–110.
2. Richard Olney, "The Growth of Our Foreign Policy," in *The Making of America,* vol. 2, ed. Robert Marion La Follette (Chicago: DeBower, Chaplin, 1907), 130.
3. Josiah Strong, *Our Country: Its Possible Future and Its Present Crisis* (New York: Baker and Taylor, 1885), 175.

13. Empire?

1. Albert Beveridge's speech in the US Senate on January 9, 1900, *Congressional Record,* 56th Congress 1st session, 704–12.
2. Rudyard Kipling, "The White Man's Burden: The United States and the Philippine Islands," *McClure's Magazine,* February 1899.

14. Nation, or World?

1. Theodore Roosevelt, "Washington's Forgotten Maxim," address before the Naval War College, June 1897, in *The Works of Theodore Roosevelt* (New York: Charles Scribner's Sons, 1906), 9:74.
2. Elihu Root, *Nobel Prize Lecture, 1912,* http://www.nobelprize.org.
3. Nicholas Murray Butler, *The International Mind: An Argument for the Judicial Settlement of International Disputes* (New York: Charles Scribner's Sons, 1912), 74.
4. David Starr Jordan, *The Call of the Nation: A Plea for Taking Politics Out of Politics* (Boston: Beacon Press, 1910), 86–87.
5. Ibid., 89.
6. Woodrow Wilson's speech before the Young Men's Christian Association, October 24, 1914, in *Selected Addresses and Papers of Woodrow Wilson* (New York: Boni and Liverlight, 1918), 49–55.

15. Pacifism vs. Peace

1. Exchange during a conference with the US Senate Foreign Relations Committee at the White House on August 19, 1919, between President Woodrow Wilson and Senator Warren Harding, quoted in Norman A. Graebner, *Ideas and Diplomacy: Readings in the Intellectual Tradition of American Foreign Policy* (New York: Oxford University Press, 1964), 485.

2. Henry L. Stimson and McGeorge Bundy, *On Active Service in Peace and War* (New York: Harper & Brothers, 1947), 232–33.

3. William E. Borah, "Public Opinion Outlaws War," *Independent* 113 September 1924): 147–49.

4. Herbert Hoover's address on Armistice Day, November 11, 1929, in *The State Papers and Other Public Writings of Herbert Hoover*, ed. William Starr Myers (Garden City, NY: Doubleday, Doran, 1934), 1:125–32.

5. Cordell Hull, "Principles of American Foreign Policy," in *Foreign Relations of the United States, 1937* (Washington, DC: US Government Printing Office, 1954), 1:699–700.

6. Franklin Roosevelt's October 5, 1937, "Quarantine Speech," http://millercenter.org/president/speeches/detail/3310.

7. Franklin Roosevelt's September 3, 1939, "There Will Be No Blackout of Peace in America" radio address, http://www.ibiblio.org/pha/policy/1939/1939-09-03a.html.

8. Franklin Roosevelt's December 29, 1940, "The Arsenal of Democracy" radio address, http://millercenter.org/president/speeches/detail/3319.

16. War for Everything, and Nothing

1. *Peace and War: United States Foreign Policy, 1931–1941* (Washington, DC: US Government Printing Office, 1943), 842–48.

2. Samuel J. Rosenman, ed., *Public Papers of Franklin D. Roosevelt* (New York: Random House, 1950), 11:41–42.

3. Charles de Gaulle, *Mémoires de Guerre* (Paris: Librairie Plon, 1954), 2:292.

4. Stimson and Bundy, *On Active Service in Peace and War,* 581.

5. John Lewis Gaddis, *George F. Kennan: An American Life* (New York: Penguin Press, 2011).

6. Robert E. Sherwood, *Roosevelt and Hopkins: An Intimate History* (New York: Harper and Brothers, 1948), 870.

7. Arthur H. Vandenberg, *Vital Speeches*, vol. 12, March 15, 1946, 322–26.

17. Cold War

1. Kevin Mooney, "Ted Kennedy's KGB Correspondence," *American Spectator*, June 10, 2010, http://spectator.org/archives/2010/06/22/ted-kennedys-kgb-correspondenc.

18. No-Win War, No Peace

1. General Omar Bradley's testimony before the Senate Committees on Armed Services and Foreign Relations, May 15, 1951, "Military Situation in the Far East" hearings, 82d Congress, 1st session, part 2, 732 (1951).

2. Murrey Marder, "Summit Clouded by Watergate," *Washington Post*, July 4, 1974, http://www.washingtonpost.com/wp-srv/inatl/longterm/summit /archive/july74.htm.

3. Bernard Gwertzman, "Marines Are Neither Combatants nor Targets, US Insists," *New York Times*, September 1, 1983, http://www.nytimes.com /1983/09/01/world/marines-are-neither-combatants-nor-targets-in-beirut-us -insists.html.

19. Peacekeeping vs. Peace

1. Niall Ferguson, *Colossus: The Price of America's Empire* (New York: The Penguin Press, 2004), 115.

2. Ibid.,121.

21. No Peace at Home

1. Charlie Savage, "Secret US Memo Made Case to Kill a Citizen," *New York Times*, October 8, 2011, http://www.nytimes.com/2011/10/09/world/middleeast /secret-us-memo-made-legal-case-to-kill-a-citizen.html?pagewanted=all&_r=0.

2. Charlie Savage and Scott Shane, "Memo Cites Legal Basis for Killing US Citizens in al Qaeda," *New York Times*, February 5, 2013, http://www.nytimes .com/2013/02/05/us/politics/us-memo-details-views-on-killing-citizens-in-al -qaeda.html.

3. John Yoo, "Courts at War," *Cornell Law Review* 91, no. 2 (2006), 583.

22. What Can Be America's Peace?

1. Barack Obama's speech to the National Defense University, May 23, 2013, http://www.whitehouse.gov.remarks.president-national-defense-university

2. Editorial page, *Wall Street Journal*, May 24, 2013, 14.

3. Shaun Waterman, "NSA chief's admission of misleading numbers adds to Obama administration blunders," *Washington Times*, October 2, 2013, http:// www.washingtontimes.com/news/2013/oct/2/nsa-chief-figures-foiled-terror -plots-misleading/?page=all.

References

Adams, Charles F., ed. *Memoirs of John Quincy Adams*. Elibron Classics, 2007.

Allen, William B., ed. *George Washington: A Collection*. Indianapolis: Liberty Fund, 1988.

Andrew, Christopher, and Alexander Gordievsky, *KGB: The Inside Story of Its Foreign Operations from Lenin to Gorbachev*. United Kingdom: Hodder & Stoughton, 1990.

Angell, Norman. *The Great Illusion: A Study of the Relation of Military Power in Nations to Their Economic and Social Advantage*. New York: Putnam, 1910.

Aquinas, Thomas. *Commentary on Aristotle's "Politics"* [1272].

———. *Summa Theologica* [1273].

Aurelia, Henry, ed. and trans. *The De Monarchia of Dante Alighieri*. Boston and New York: Houghton, Mifflin, 1904.

Basler, Roy P., et al., eds. *The Collected Works of Abraham Lincoln*. New Brunswick, NJ: Rutgers University Press, 1953.

Bergson, Henri. *Creative Evolution* [*L'Évolution creatice*, 1907]. New York: MacMillan, 1911.

Bernhardi, Friedrich von. *Germany and the Next War*. Translated by Allan H. Fowles. New York: Longmans, Green, 1914.

Beveridge, Albert J. *In Support of an American Empire*. January 9, 1900. http://teachingamericanhistory.org/library/document/in-support-of-an-american-empire.

Blaine, James G. *Twenty Years of Congress: From Lincoln to Garfield*. Norwich, CT: Henry Bill, 1886.

Bolingbroke, Henry St. John. *The Idea of a Patriot King*. December 1, 1738. http://socserv2.socsci.mcmaster.ca/~econ/ugcm/3ll3/bolingbroke/king.html.

Borah, William. "Public Opinion Outlaws War." *Independent* 113 (September 1924): 147–49.

Bostom, Andrew G. *Sharia Versus Freedom: The Legacy of Islamic Totalitarianism*. Amherst, NY: Prometheus Books, 2012.

Brodie, Bernard, ed. *The Absolute Weapon: Atomic Power and World Order.* New York: Harcourt, 1946.

Butler, Nicholas Murray. *The International Mind: An Argument for the Judicial Settlement of International Disputes.* New York: Charles Scribner's Sons, 1913.

Butler, Samuel, trans., and James H. Ford, ed. *Homer: The Iliad and The Odyssey* [8th century BC]. El Paso, TX: El Paso Norte Press, 2006.

Codevilla, Angelo M. *Advice to War Presidents: A Remedial Course in Statecraft.* New York: Basic Books, 2009.

———. *No Victory, No Peace.* Lanham, MD: Rowman & Littlefield, 2005.

Codevilla, Angelo M., and Paul Seabury. *War: Ends and Means.* Dulles, VA: Potomac Books, 2006 [revised].

Cohn, Norman O. *The Pursuit of the Millennium: Revolutionary Millenarians and Mystical Anarchists of the Middle Ages.* New York: Oxford University Press, 1970.

Crapol, Edward P. *James G. Blaine: Architect of Empire.* Wilmington, DE: Scholarly Resources, 2000.

Dods, Marcus, trans. *The City of God: Saint Augustine.* Peabody, MA: Hendrickson, 2009.

Dulles, John Foster. *War or Peace.* New York: Macmillan, 1950.

———. *War, Peace, and Change.* New York: Harper and Row, 1939.

Ford, Worthington C., ed. *The Writings of John Quincy Adams.* 7 vols. New York, 1913–17.

Fortescue, John. *De Laudibus Legum Angliae* [1471]. Cambridge: Cambridge University Press, 1949.

Friedman, Thomas. *The Lexus and the Olive Tree: Understanding Globalization.* New York: Picador, 1999.

Gaddis, John Lewis. *George F. Kennan: An American Life.* New York: Penguin Press, 2011.

Gardiner, William Howard. "A Naval View of the Conference." *Atlantic Monthly* 129 (April 1922): 522–39.

Gibbon, Edward. *The Decline and Fall of the Roman Empire* [1776)]. United Kingdom: Wordsworth Editions, 1998.

Gilbert, Felix. *To the Farewell Address: Ideas of American Foreign Policy.* Princeton, NJ: Princeton University Press, 1961.

Graebner, Norman A. *Ideas and Diplomacy: Readings in the Intellectual Tradition of American Foreign Policy.* New York: Oxford University Press, 1964.

Grew, Robert C. *Turbulent Era: A Diplomatic Record of Forty Years, 1904–1945.* Boston: Houghton Mifflin, 1952.

Hill, David Jayne. "A Question of Honor." *North American Review* 212 (October 1920): 433–48.

Hull, Cordell. *The Memoirs of Cordell Hull.* New York; McMillan, 1948.

Jaffa, Harry V. *Crisis of the House Divided: An Interpretation of the Issues of the Lincoln-Douglas Debate.* Chicago: University of Chicago Press, 1958.

Jefferson, Thomas. *A Summary View of the Rights of British America* [1774]. New York: Lenox Hill, 1971.

Johnson, Paul. *Modern Times: The World from the Twenties to the Nineties.* New York: Harper and Row, 1983.

Jordan, David Starr. *The Blood of the Nation: A Study of the Decay of Races through the Survival of the Unfit.* Boston: American Unitarian Association, 1902.

———— *War and Waste: A Series of Discussions of War and War Accessories.* New York: Doubleday, 1913.

Kahn, Herman. *On Thermonuclear War.* Princeton, NJ: Princeton University Press, 1960.

Kennan, George F. *Memoirs, 1950–1963.* Boston: Little, Brown, 1967.

Kipling, Rudyard. *Recessional* [1897].

Kissinger, Henry. *Diplomacy.* New York: Simon and Schuster, 1994.

————. *The Necessity for Choice: Prospects of American Foreign Policy.* New York: Harper and Row, 1961.

————. *Nuclear Weapons and Foreign Policy.* Council on Foreign Relations, 1957.

Kleiman, Robert. *Atlantic Crisis: American Diplomacy Confronts a Resurgent Europe.* New York: W. W. Norton, 1964.

Lansing, Robert. "The Effort to Outlaw War." *Independent* (August 1924).

Mably, Gabriel Bonnot de. *On the Principles of Negotiations in the Service of International Law Founded on Treaties* [1757].

MacArthur, Douglas. *Reminiscences.* New York: McGraw-Hill, 1964.

Mahan, Alfred Thayer. *The Influence of Sea Power upon History: 1660–1783* [1890]. Boston: Little, Brown, 1918.

Mango, Andrew. *Atatürk: The Biography of the Founder of Modern Turkey.* London: John Murray, 1999.

Mann, James. *The Obamians: The Struggle inside the White House to Redefine American Power.* New York: Penguin Group, 2012.

————. *The Rise of the Vulcans: The History of Bush's War Cabinet.* New York: Penguin Group, 2004.

Marsilius of Padua, *Defensor Pacis* [The Defender of Peace, 1324].

McDougall, Walter A. *Freedom Just around the Corner: A New American History, 1585–1828.* New York: Harper Collins, 2004.

————. *Promised Land, Crusader State: The American Encounter with the World since 1776.* New York: Houghton Mifflin Harcourt, 1997.

————. *Throes of Democracy: The American Civil War Era, 1829–1877.* New York: Harper, 2008.

McNamara, Robert S. *In Retrospect: The Tragedy and Lessons of Vietnam.* New York: Times Books, 1995.

Montesquieu. *The Greatness of the Romans and Their Decline* [1735]. Translated by David Lowenthal. Ithaca, NY: Cornell University Press, 1968.

Nevins, Allan, ed. *The Diary of John Quincy Adams, 1794–1845: American Diplomacy, and Political, Social, and Intellectual Life, from Washington to Polk.* New York: Charles Scribner's Sons, 1951.

Nietzsche, Friedrich. *Beyond Good and Evil* [1886]. Translated by Helen Zimmern. Madison, WI: Cricket House Books, 2012.

———. *The Will to Power* [1885]. Translated by Walter Kaufmann and R. J. Hollingdale. Edited by Walter Kaufmann. New York: Vintage Books, 1967.

Paine, Thomas. *Common Sense* [1776], http://www.ushistory.org/paine/common sense/sense1.htm.

Paulus Diaconus [Paul the Deacon]. *History of the Longobards* [circa AD 780]. Philadelphia: University of Pennsylvania, 1907.

Publius [Alexander Hamilton, James Madison, John Jay]. *Federalist* [1789], http://thomas.loc.gov/home/histdox/fedpapers.html.

Reilly, Robert. *The Closing of the Muslim Mind: How Intellectual Suicide Created the Modern Islamist Crisis*. Wilmington, DE: Intercollegiate Studies Institute, 2010.

Roosevelt, Franklin D. *Speeches*. Charlottesville: Miller Center, University of Virginia, http://millercenter.org/president/speeches.

Roosevelt, Theodore. *Addresses and Presidential Messages of Theodore Roosevelt, 1902–1904*. New York: G. P. Putnam's Sons, 1904.

———. *America and the World War*. New York: Charles Scribner's Sons, 1915.

———. *Selections from the Correspondence of Theodore Roosevelt and Henry Cabot Lodge, 1884–1918*. New York: Da Capo Press, 1971.

———. *The Letters of Theodore Roosevelt*. Edited by Elting E. Morison. Cambridge, MA: Harvard University Press, 1951.

———. *The Naval War of 1812*. New York: G. P. Putnam's Sons, 1882.

Root, Elihu. *Addresses on International Subjects*. Edited by Robert Bacon and James Brown Scott. Cambridge, MA: Harvard University Press, 1916.

———. *Nobel Prize Lecture, 1912*. http://www.nobelprize.org.

Sandoz, Ellis, ed. *Political Sermons of the American Founding Era, 1730–1805*. Indianapolis, IN: Liberty Press, 1991.

Schelling, Thomas C. *The Strategy of Conflict*. Cambridge, MA: Harvard University Press, 1960.

Sherwood, Robert E. *Roosevelt and Hopkins: An Intimate History*. New York: Harper, 1949.

Stephens, Alexander H. *A Compendium of the History of the United States: From the Earliest Settlements to 1883*. New York: E. J. Hale & Son, 1889.

Stimson, Henry, and McGeorge Bundy. *On Active Service in Peace and War*. New York: Harper & Brothers, 1947.

Strong, Josiah. *Our Country: Its Possible Future and Its Present Crisis*. New York: American Home Missionary Society, 1885.

Summers, Harry G. *On Strategy: A Critical Analysis of the Vietnam War*. New York: Presidio Press, 1982.

Taft, Robert A. *A Foreign Policy for Americans*. New York: Doubleday, 1951.

Thucydides. *History of the Peloponnesian War* [5th century BC]. Translated by Rex Warner. United Kingdom: Penguin Books, 1954.

Tuchman, Barbara W. *The Guns of August*. New York: Random House, 1962.

Turgot, Anne-Robert-Jacques. *Reflections on the Formation and Distribution of Wealth* [1766].

Williams, William Appleman. *The Tragedy of American Diplomacy.* Cleveland: World Publishing, 1959.

Wilson, Woodrow. *Congressional Government: A Study in American Politics* [1885]. Boston: Houghton Mifflin, 1901. And addresses: "The Opinion of the World" (1914), "The Power of Christian Young Men" (1914), "A World League for Peace" (1917), "Reply to Pope" (1917).

Yoo, John. *Crisis and Command: A History of Executive Power from George Washington to George W. Bush.* New York: Kaplan, 2010.

———. *The Powers of War and Peace: The Constitution and Foreign Affairs after 9/11.* Chicago: University of Chicago Press, 2005.

———. *War by Other Means: An Insider's Account of the War on Terror.* New York: Atlantic Monthly Press, 2006.

About the Author

Angelo M. Codevilla is a professor emeritus of international relations at Boston University, a member of the Hoover Institution's working group on military history, and a fellow of the Claremont Institute. He was a US naval officer and Foreign Service officer and served on the staff of the Senate Intelligence Committee as well as on presidential transition teams. Formerly a senior research fellow at the Hoover Institution, he is the author of thirteen books, including *War: Ends and Means*, *Informing Statecraft*, *The Ruling Class*, *The Character of Nations*, *Advice to War Presidents*, and *A Student's Guide to International Relations*. His essays and op-eds, written in several languages, have appeared in major domestic and foreign magazines and newspapers. He is a student of the classics. Married since 1966, he has raised five children and now raises wine grapes commercially.

WORKING GROUP ON THE ROLE OF
MILITARY HISTORY IN CONTEMPORARY CONFLICT

The Working Group on the Role of Military History in Contemporary
Conflict has set its agenda mindful of the Hoover Institution's dedication to historical research in light of contemporary challenges and,
in particular, reinvigorating the national study of military history to
foster and enhance our national security.

Chaired by Hoover senior fellow Victor Davis Hanson with counsel
from Hoover research fellows Bruce Thornton and David Berkey,
along with collaboration from the group's distinguished scholars,
military historians, security analysts, journalists, and military vet-
erans and practitioners, this team examines how knowledge of past
military operations can influence contemporary public policy decisions concerning current conflicts. The careful study of military history offers a way to analyze modern war and peace that is often
underappreciated in this age of technological determinism. The result
of such study is an in-depth and dispassionate understanding of contemporary wars, one that explains how particular military successes
and failures of the past can be often germane, sometimes misunder-
stood, or occasionally irrelevant in the context of the present.

Index